# How to Advance Your Career in Professional Services Marketing

## BE MORE PURPOSEFUL AND STRATEGIC WITH YOUR CAREER DIRECTION

# Dominic Ayres

# Acknowledgements

Writing a book is more challenging than I thought and more rewarding than ever imagined. None of this would have been possible without my family, colleagues and friends for your help producing this book.

Having a good line manager and mentors to help you develop and grow in your career is essential to advancing your career in the professional services industry. Special thanks to the following managers, mentors and colleagues who have helped me in my career development. Your advice and guidance over the last 12 years have been instrumental.

Kate Marsden
Zelinda Bennett
Ranjit Dhillion
Andrew Warren
Rich Smith
Daniel Tompsett
Paul Taylor
Courtney Borthwick
Dal Banwait
Ian Cohn

Of course, there is a more comprehensive list of colleagues and stakeholders I have worked with within my career who have also directly influenced this book in some form or another.

I would also like to thank the collection of experts around the globe, many of whom I knew prior to writing the book, and many that I have connected through the creation of this book. Each of you have brought some fantastic insight into your own career journey and offered the reader practical guidance to help them in their career journey. Each of you have brought the content in this book to life for the reader:

Adriana Giometti

Alexander Low

Alistair Brisbourne

Andrew Katznelson

Annette Morgan

Astrid Altmann Forbes

Barbara Koenen-Geerdink

Ben Kent

Bridget Uebel

Carolyn Manning

Charlotte Sansom

Chris Saul

Claire Rason

Dal Banwait

Daniel Shaw

Daniel Tompsett

Deborah Brightman Farone

Deborah Macrae

Elvis Yarda

Eva Wisnik

Frances Haughey

Gina Rubel

Hannah Smith-Pickup

Hannah Taylor

Harriet Lake

Heather Reid

Heidi K. Gardner

Hugo Pena

Ian Cohn

Jamie Wallis

Jeff Berardi

Jeremy Ford

Kate Harry Shipham

Katy Foster

Keith Hardie

Koree Khongphand-Buckman

Kristel van den Elzen

Kristian Joyce

Laura Ottley

Leor Franks

Lindsay Griffiths

Lucy Canning

Luke Ferrandino

Matthew Gardner

Naomi Rendell

Nora Shearer

Paul Taylor

Peter Kane

Rachel Kennedy

Rahul Gossain

Rebecca Wright

Rhys Calcott

Richard Grove

Roy Sexton

Sadie Baron

Si Marshall

Steve Blundell

Stuart J T Dodds

Tamara Box

Tim Corcoran

Tis Dias

Verity Jackson-Grant

William Walder

Zelinda Bennett

# Foreword

I have spent nearly twenty years working in the professional services industry, which feels incredibly long in retrospect. During my career, I've worked for some fantastic organisations such as Linklaters, Slaughter and May, Ashurst and now AlixPartners across strategy, business management, marketing, and business development. I have been fortunate enough to work across Asia, Australia, the United States and Europe, which has given me the unique opportunity to travel to different places and work with people from different cultures and backgrounds.

I graduated from Leeds University with a degree in Medical Science. I majored in pharmaceuticals, with the ultimate goal of working for a big pharma company. After graduating, I completed a master's degree in Marketing and Business Management (with 1st class honours) before getting my first graduate role at BOC (now part of The Linde Group). The reason for this background information? It nicely demonstrates that those working in the industry come from diverse backgrounds and education.

Despite having had, what I consider, to be a pretty good career to date, I didn't set out to build a career in professional services marketing as my number one career choice? Absolutely not. Nobody does. And anybody that says they do is a liar. Let's be honest with one another. We would much rather have got a dream job at Unilever or Adidas. This job ultimately chooses you. Having set out to work in something far more glamorous, I wouldn't change anything (most things) about how my career has played out in the industry.

Over those twenty years, I've worked with some fantastic colleagues and professionals, none more so than Dominic. For as long as I've known Dominic, he's been passionate and disciplined about professional development. From our early interactions about the usefulness of data and Excel (yes, marketing people need to know how to use Excel and PowerPoint) to conversations about elevating relationships with partners so that we (marketing and business development professionals) operate as strategic advisors. Throughout this time, he has been determined to advance his knowledge base, develop his career and further those who work with him, and, more recently, the broader professional services marketing and business development community.

This book lays out the foundations for anybody that wants to succeed in professional services marketing. Not only will you learn from Dominic's insights gathered from over 12 years in the industry, but you will also gain insight from leaders across the profession who have had highly successful careers and have probably learnt these lessons the hard way. It's also a book that you can come back to repeatedly, revisiting the fundamentals of being a marketing leader and elevating yourself to a 'strategic advisor' within your firm. Dominic's approach is practical and straightforward, and as well as providing excellent views and opinions, he also provides supporting materials to help you structure your thinking.

I've always been passionate about the development of people, the enhancement of teams and the elevation of marketing and business development functions within professional services organisations. They are hugely rewarding places to work, and your career can thrive within them. This book is excellent for newcomers to the industry, those who think they've plateaued within their career, and those wanting to advance their career. Finally, it's great for seasoned CMOs that might have forgotten what it was once like when they first joined a professional services organisation. It will support you in building and coaching highly motivated and successful teams.

PAUL TAYLOR
Director and Head of Business Development (EMEA)
AlixPartners

# Introduction

*"In real life, strategy is actually very straightforward.*
*You pick a general direction and implement like hell"*
*—Jack Welch*

## Why should you read this book?

As the Chinese proverb goes, *"The best time to plant a tree was 20 years ago. The second best time is now."* So whether you're at the start of your professional services marketing career or further along, now is the time to begin being proactive in how you manage and develop your career.

Getting ahead requires thinking strategically, embodying specific values to help you stand out amongst your peers, and successfully navigating whilst building relationships with internal stakeholders, and managing your career proactively.

The problem is that firms develop their Marketing teams in an ad-hoc way without a clear roadmap to where they want you to grow. Formal objectives and appraisals are helpful, but they don't condition-specific behaviour, develop knowledge, and the skills essential for your career growth within the industry.

It's also difficult and expensive to find resources that teach these lessons. Professional service books are some of the most expensive books on Amazon. Furthermore, they are often devoid of practical application and not relevant for those who work in the industry.

As you progress into senior positions the level of supervision and guidance you have will diminish, meaning your development is primarily reliant upon yourself going forwards. Because Marketing departments in professional service firms often have flat structures, this only intensifies the level of internal and external competition you will face when seeking new positions.

The only person who is going to advance your career is you.

Take it from someone who has worked in the professional services industry since 2009 and progressed from a Marketing Assistant to senior management. I was introduced to the world of professional services marketing as part of my marketing degree at University when I underwent a year-long placement at global law firm DLA Piper in 2009. After graduating from University, I worked at Slaughter and May, a Magic Circle firm (an informal term describing the five most prestigious London-headquartered multinational law firms) for several years, progressing from junior roles into more senior positions. Most recently, I have advanced my career from a manager position into my current role, which is a senior management position at Eversheds Sutherland, a global multinational law practice.

Over the last 12 years, I have used and tested the advice and lessons outlined in this book and passed them onto those I have mentored and managed. This book is what I wish someone had written and handed me during my placement year at DLA Piper and in the earlier years of my career.

## Who is this book for?

Designed to contain everything you will need to know and implement in your career, whether you are just starting your marketing career in the professional services industry, working towards senior roles or a seasoned CMO. Depending on what stage you are at in your career, this book includes insights, ideas and practical guidance for you to use in your career.

## The purpose of this book

There are good books on marketing and good books on career management - but not one that has brought these two topics together in the professional services industry for marketing professionals until now. This book aims to create a practical guide for you and others aspiring to progress their career in the industry.

There are many opportunities to advance and challenges to avoid, so taking a proactive and strategic approach in your career will be critical to your success. With the help of this book, you will become more strategic with your career progression, and you'll learn how you can think differently, take action, and utilise specific tools and processes to develop yourself and your career.

## How should you use this book?

This book is your very own career manual, full of ideas and guidance to help you advance your career. Look upon this as a source of reassurance and inspiration when you feel stuck or have challenges to overcome to progress your career. Structured into succinct chapters and sections, which means you can easily reread and look up parts of the book when you need specific guidance or information on a challenge you are trying to overcome.

This book is structured in a way that helps you to be more strategic with your career direction, work more effectively in a team, manage internal stakeholders and proactively manage your career. It is designed to be easy-to-read and used, picked up or put down as needed or read from beginning to end in a short amount of time. It only contains a range of advice, tools and behaviour I have utilised to advance my career in the industry.

I have shared my own career experience throughout the book and explained how I had applied many of the advice and behaviours outlined in this book to advance my career. These sections are labelled *"in practice"* throughout the book.

Further to my own experience and guidance, I have sought the best minds from across the industry worldwide to share their guidance and case studies on how they have developed their career and recommendations for you to follow in your career. These professionals hold senior, director and CMO positions at some of the largest professional services firms such as the Big4, AM100, Magic Circle and other leading firms. In addition, I have gathered a wider perspective from recruiters and senior partners. These sections are labelled *"expert view"* throughout the book.

## It comprises five parts:

- **Part one: Making an impact in your career** - whether you have just started your career in the industry or are moving roles to advance your career, this part of the book shares a 90-day recommendations plan that will equip you with practical strategies and steps to make an impact in your new role. It also defines what it takes to become a CMO and what is expected of future CMO's in the future.
- **Part two: Alignment with your firm's strategy** - provides insights and ideas on what behaviours you should be implementing in your role to transition from focusing only on the tactical aspects of your position to leading the firm's strategic direction when it comes to marketing.
- **Part three: Working together as a team** - guides you on how to manage your colleagues' expectations and identify the best processes and resources to deliver marketing initiatives. It also prepares you for when you step up into a more senior role where you have to manage a team toward a specific objective.
- **Part four: Internal stakeholder management** - covers practical advice on developing your internal brand and reputation. Also,

manage and meet senior stakeholders' needs to meet your objectives and advance your promotional prospects.

- **Part five: Proactive career management** - provides ideas and insight into developing yourself continuously. Also, learn how to cultivate your external connections and manage your brand within the industry.

To help you go out there and begin using the guidance in this book, you will find key points to consider at the end of each chapter that summarises what you need to start doing to develop yourself and your career.

## Bonus Material - Continuous learning

There are many new information sources you can seek out in searching for ongoing knowledge and skill development. Specific technical skills and areas of expertise are essential to progressing your career in the professional services industry. I have compiled a list of my recommended reading to help you build up your knowledge in key areas you need in your career.

I have also built a list of resources I review regularly and a list of essential industry know-how, ranging from podcasts, articles, and videos you should familiarise yourself with.

## Templates and Tools

To help you get out there and begin using the guidance in this book, I have developed several templates and additional materials that you can access for free, alongside the bonus chapter.

Please email: dominicayresbook@gmail.com with the subject bar 'Bonus Materials' to access these materials.

# Contents

# PART ONE

# Making an impact in your career

*"Dreams are extremely important. You can't do it unless you imagine it"*
*—George Lucas*

Marketing roles within the professional services industry are unlike any other marketing endeavour your education or prior experience has likely come across or prepared you for a career in . There is a reason you will often hear how difficult it is to start a career in the professional services marketing industry and why it is a mandatory requirement to possess the specific experience to take on a role in the industry.

As most marketing resources are based internally, you can gain exposure to various marketing disciplines within firms. Allowing you to discover what you are passionate about at the beginning of your career and the opportunity to hone your technical skills across various essential areas. As a result of the team structure, if you are interested in specialising further down the road, you can do so.

Business Development and Marketing roles in the industry offer a rewarding career platform for aspiring marketers because they involve a variety of exciting and diverse challenges. However, it isn't an obvious career choice for many upon graduation or changing careers.

To develop a successful career in the industry, it is vital that you understand it and how it compares to others to begin building a career in the industry. This section of the book helps you navigate from starting in the industry to reaching the top.

# 1

# Launching your career in professional services marketing

*"You take the blue pill... the story ends, you wake up in your bed and believe whatever you want to believe. You take the red pill... you stay in Wonderland, and I show you how deep the rabbit hole goes"*
—Morpheus

You are considering a career in professional services marketing or have recently moved into the industry from a B2C organisation. In that case, you must understand some of the critical differences to adapt and develop your career in the industry.

## Products and services

A particular challenge for professional services firms is that the *"product"* is usually the people providing the service (intangible). Unlike most marketing degrees that focus on tangible products, often in a B2C environment, the professional services industry is more challenging because advisors are tasked with marketing and creating opportunities to advise clients. Additionally, you will interact with various stakeholders with different ideas and expertise.

The advisors you work with are often highly educated and sought after by their clients for their high-quality and complex advice. Therefore, creating the expectations internally must deliver relevant, fast-paced, and accurate output.

The industry and the stigma surrounding it, to outsiders, initially appears scary and strict. Learn from people in your firm and work with them on initiatives by getting to know them. Later in the book, we will cover working with stakeholders [see PART FOUR].

---

## Expert view

Kristian Joyce, Head of Business Development (Asia Pacific) at Aon, based in Australia:

---

*"Starting in the professional services industry can often be quite a daunting experience: plenty of exceptionally bright people, many of whom are rewarded for accuracy and tend to be perfectionists. As with most roles, initial success often depends on your ability to build rapport and understand the business.*

*But this is not as easy as it sounds. Genuinely understanding the business involves you proactively investing your time, for instance, meeting with stakeholders and understanding the anatomy of a deal, the dynamics of how the client, the adviser, and other parties interact, and how this activity is measured and rewarded within the firm.*

*Equipped with this knowledge, you can begin to understand how all the pieces fit together and add plenty of value, regardless of whether your role is in the business development, marketing, client management space or a mix.*

*My journey began 24 years ago, and I am still learning plenty every year."*

---

## Market and competition

In this sector, the pace is often fast, and the complexity is high in the industry. Market competition is fierce, and clients demand services delivered by tight deadlines. Understanding client demands for these various service areas is crucial to your role in your firm [see CHAPTER 6]. It is essential to be flexible and adaptable to the constantly changing demands of clients and the business world to cope with and rise to the challenge.

Typically no two days in the industry are the same, whether you're working on a pitch opportunity that alters your list of planned priorities for the day or tackling a marketing push to help a particular product area position itself in the market. Unlike B2C, where there can often be only one marketing campaign per year, the industry usually has multiple campaigns running simultaneously. You are exposed to a wide range of business facets in your role, which can help you stay motivated and keep your interest in the industry high.

___

**Expert view**  Leor Franks, Business Development & Marketing Director at Kingsley Napley and Author of The Favourability Journey®, based in London:

*"Most marketers I've worked with over the past 20-years in professional services think about target clients when putting together BD plans. There is, however, often a lack of rigour in identifying exactly how a target perceives your firm and, therefore, what marketing investments would be most effective in improving this view. The Favourability Journey tool can help bridge this gap. This approach considers the four stages of a target's journey with a firm, described as the four Rs: Recognition, Reputation, Relationships, and Revenue.*

*Imagine meeting a new client for a drink to bring the approach to life:*

1.  *Recognition. You arrive early at the bar. Considering what to order, you see 30 bottles on the shelf; none are known to you. How can you select without any brand recognition? Looking closely, eight are from a region you are familiar with. You've reached the first stage of the Favourability Journey: 'Recognition'. But without further data, eight is too many to select from.*

2.  *Reputation. There are no staff in sight, so you cheekily hop behind the bar and examine the eight. Without any information on the quality of*

*these, how do you pick? Four of the bottles proudly display an award logo. This gives you the sense that they are of decent calibre. You've hit the second stage of the Favourability Journey: 'Reputation'. Still, four is too many to select from.*

3.  *Relationships. A barkeeper greets you. They chat about your likes/ dislikes. They suggest that two of the four bottles would be to your taste with this insight. You've arrived at the third stage of the Favourability Journey: 'Relationships'. Two is a practical range to pick from, but what about the price tag?*

4.  *Revenue. The waiter says one bottle is £75 and the other, £20. You pause to think about what will work with your client - the pricey, flashy bottle or the cheaper bargain basement choice. You've landed at the final stage of the Favourability Journey: 'Revenue'. Worried about your firm's bribery rules, you go for the lower-priced option! In minutes, you've journeyed from unengaged and unaware, without Recognition of any brands, to gain an insight on Reputations. With advice based on a Relationship, you've taken an educated decision to provide Revenue to one of the brands. This journey is potentially familiar for individual purchases of products. It may also relate to the type of journey targets go through with professional service firms .*

*Knowing where a client is on their journey with your practice is the first step to making the right marketing investment decisions."*

## Customers

Knowing your customers is vital particularly when firms offer intabile products as discussed. When you're selling something that is difficult for customers to understand or conceptualise, knowing their needs is increasingly important.

In the same way, your international stakeholders are highly educated, and your clients are highly educated as well. Clients require relevant knowledge of your firm's services when they require assistance from your firm. They want information and know-how to make significant decisions for their organisations, where content marketing comes into the picture.

Professional service firms target several vital decision-makers within an organisation instead of B2C companies who can target anyone who can use their products or services, not necessarily the buyer. The target audience expectations in the B2B sector focus on efficiency and expertise. In contrast, audiences in the B2C industry are more likely to be seeking deals and entertainment, which means the professional services sector's audience is driven more by logic and financial incentive (ROI).

Despite a small number of buyers to focus on in the target organisation, the chain of command is longer with procurement, accounting, and department heads often needing to approve purchases in B2B situations. There is a much longer B2B buying cycle than B2C purchases. In B2B marketing, nurturing leads and paying attention to user experience is essential.

The industry has many unique and challenging nuances to overcome as a professional. The opportunity to build a long and rewarding career in a single industry is possible, which might not be possible in B2C industries. You might move from one industry to another drastically differently, from automotive to medical devices. Therefore, you should understand the above characteristics when you start your career and adjust your approach to your new role.

---

## Expert view

Bridget Uebel, Global Chief Marketing and Business Development Officer at Hausfeld, based in London:

---

*"As you progress your career in a law firm or professional services partnership environment, there are a few things that will help along the way:*

*Get to know your 'internal' and 'external' clients. As a marketing and business development professional and effectively part of a business services team, you have two sets of clients to support. Your internal clients (partners) and advisors that you work with, and your 'external' clients – the clients that the firm services. Both have different needs, but you need to understand both to succeed. At a more junior level, your priority will be getting to know and meeting the needs of your 'internal' clients. Your manager will be able to help you with that. As your career grows and you develop a good understanding of your firm's different product areas, you may want to consider spending some time in a client development role. Allowing you to take a much deeper dive into understanding how clients operate and, with time and experience, you will be able to gain direct client-facing experience.*

*My first client-facing role was at Freshfields. In my first week, a senior stakeholder tasked me to determine who was responsible for internal technical training at a portfolio of clients. Once I had discovered who those contacts were, my objective was to build relationships and training programmes with these key clients. The project required tenacity, talking and listening to lots of different internal and external client contacts, trying to understand how their in-house training programmes worked and looking for ways to partner and engage. Clients made time to meet me to share insights into hot topics that similar clients were facing. With regular client interaction and ensuring that I was keeping up to speed with each client's business, I began to be seen as the 'go to' internal contact by partners and advisors across the network for everything to do with the clients in the sector I was supporting.*

*Working in a partnership environment can be challenging, so you must balance strategic thinking with execution in your role. As a marketing and business development professional, you have to balance the needs of multiple 'business owners' (all the equity partners) in addition to the focus of your marketing and business development team. As I've developed my career in the industry, I've learned that advisors wear multiple business 'hats' – from managing and leading a business/practice area or office/ region, to advising clients, to supporting and training a team, to marketing themselves and their specialism, to identifying, developing and winning business, to maintaining excellent client relationships, as well as all the other responsibilities that come from being in a partnership structured business. Wearing such a range of different 'hats' requires enormous flexibility, tenacity, and the ability to be both strategic and operational, as well as entrepreneurial. What a combination of responsibilities, most of which often come with very little training or guidance along the way! Gaining credibility in your career requires understanding and mirroring some of those 'hats'. The ability to successfully execute and deliver on projects is just as crucial as any strategic advice or insights you might offer. You need to work up and down the strategic/operational scale to succeed."*

## Engaging stakeholders

Marketing and business development professionals need to manage stakeholders to be successful. Firms in the professional services sector are complex organisations that require you to interact, work, collaborate, and build relationships with internal stakeholders [see **CHAPTER 13**].

In contrast to other industries, senior stakeholders can influence your work priorities. To be effective in your role, you must gain the buy-in of these stakeholders [see **CHAPTER 14**].

To advance your career and develop trust with these stakeholders [see **CHAPTER 7**], you shouldn't simply carry out the task at hand without questioning or trying to understand their objectives.

**Expert view**   Steve Blundell, Head of Acritas Advisors at Thomson Reuters, based in London:

*"Most people who decide to work in marketing in professional services do so because they genuinely want to add value to the client experience. Most are predisposed to be 'people pleasers' – which is excellent for*

anticipating and responding to clients' needs externally - but it doesn't always help with knowing how best to add value internally to stakeholders.

Commonly, marketers start by jumping into every request or opportunity to help - and sometimes end up trapped by becoming the go-to "busy fool". So my recommendations when starting your career in the professional services sector, having made these mistakes and watched others do the same is:

- Work out what value your firm needs to add to the client experience and make sure you contribute consistently - even while you have to handle a range of tasks that likely don't!

- Make sure you find ways to interface with clients directly don't get stuck in the back office. Do some client feedback interviews or bring clients into a meeting with advisors to talk about their business.

- Remember to market yourself and your team internally, keep on telling the partners about the value you're adding and how you have helped other stakeholders achieve success.

- Bring in the very best advisors/agencies to your initiatives where needed. A good choice will always make you look good with your stakeholders."

## Career landscape

*"The organization must take care to avoid putting these marketing people in what they perceive to be dead-end positions"*

—Paul Bloom

Building a career in professional services marketing has come a long way from the earlier perceptions highlighted above many years ago. Today, firms battle for the latest talent in the industry and this is not just limited to advisors now, with marketing professionals equally in high demand.

There has never been a better time to join the industry than now.

**Expert view**     Kate Harry Shipham, Principal of KHS People, an
executive search firm placing business developers
and marketers into professional services firms
based in Chicago:

*The CMO role in a professional services firm is highly complex and far-reaching. Their role has never been more visible and open to criticism, and their role has also never been as influential and wide-reaching. They need a phenomenal team to help them further the firm's BD and marketing purpose.*

*Today, professionals in the industry need to navigate firms and all the roadblocks within them, understand the mindset of a partner and what value means to them, and have the inclination and intellectual capacity to be idea creators. These days, most firms are full of partners who want these ideas brought to them. Additionally, most professionals know how to introduce an initiative or course-correct that is needed to be more nuanced.*

*This is significantly different to past years. It used to be the case that professionals were judged solely on their technical skills and expected to feel grateful for being at the firm, and it was one-sided. Now, firms are thankful to have marketing professionals and have to engage with the market proactively, communicate their messaging on the role and team, and be prepared to answer questions from candidates on the firm's leadership, ownership, reporting lines and structures, relative progressiveness to their peers, and diversity initiatives. Once these questions are asked, the working arrangement in this current environment is next on their minds. The quality of their work and the quality of their life for marketers in the professional services industry has, generally speaking, superseded title, pay and prestige.*

*Today's professionals are judged on their cultural fit and ability to understand and accept that firms are nuanced and every detail matters. Firms want intelligent professionals who have the experience and confidence to converse with needed partners and work around hurdles. Technical skills are a given, their efficiency when working and their constant communication and expectation setting and management are critical. BD and marketing professionals are now problem solvers and business solutions focused. They have a thorough understanding of their firm and partners and are focused on the big and small picture.*

*As we move forward, I foresee these marketing professionals will be less segmented behind the scenes and reputed as established and experienced parts of the organisation. There will be a move to have less delineation between the non-fee earning professionals traditionally behind the scenes. Today, they are visible, critical problem solvers."*

 **Key points to remember**

1. Your biggest ongoing challenge as you develop your career in this industry is understanding your firm's products and services and relevance for clients, so focus on learning about them in order to thrive in your role.

2. To adapt and cope with the ever-changing demands of clients and the business world, you must be flexible and change with it.

3. Target audiences in the B2B sector often demand efficiency and expertise. In contrast, audiences in the B2C industry are more likely to seek deals and entertainment than the professional services industry audience, which focuses on logic and financial incentive (ROI).

4. Successful business development and marketing professionals need to manage stakeholders. You must interact, work, collaborate, and build relationships with internal stakeholders in your firm.

# 2

# Making an impact
# in your new role

*"Only undertake what you can do in an excellent fashion.*
*There are no prizes for average performance"*
*—Brian Tracy*

The professional services industry has evolved over recent years. Traditionally, you might have a stable and linear career path with various internal promotions within the same firm for ten years plus. Increasingly, this is becoming a thing of the past, as the market becomes highly competitive and short of candidates, impacting firms' abilities to acquire and retain the best talent available.

Firms are now investing in new headcount across the Marketing team, according to Ambition's Market Trends Q2 2021 report. With a focus on developing extra capacity or bolstering specialist areas. If you are looking to progress into senior positions in the industry outside of your current firm, this bodes well as this looks set to continue long into the future.

Changing firms is always tricky, as you will need to build up your knowledge of the firm, develop internal stakeholder relationships and your reputation from nothing. The first 90 days in a new role are exhilarating, challenging, and learning orientated. You will find yourself being dropped into a team, working with demanding stakeholders who do not know you, unfamiliar processes. You have a boss with high expectations and will need you to drive value quickly. You have peers and other functions across the firm critical to your success, also whom you need to work with effectively to achieve success in your position.

Therefore before starting your new role, you should prepare as much as possible and when you officially start, have a well-developed plan of action to ensure you settle in as quickly as possible and get off to a good start. Following the below, the 90-day guide will equip you with practical strategies and steps to ensure you make an impact in your new role.

## PREPARE [Days -30 to 0]

- **Starting in the right way** - reach out ahead to begin understanding your induction plan, so you know what is planned for your arrival and where you will need to take action to organise parts of your onboarding process yourself. Do not be surprised if your induction is limited to a few meetings or non-existent; if this is the case, this only further emphasises the need for you to take control and plan your approach before joining.

- **Clarify role expectations** - review the job description from when you were applying and interviewing for the role. Seek to communicate with your new manager to further define your responsibilities and objectives. Being clear on your expectations is critical to starting in your new position as it will help you plan accordingly and give you clear priorities to work towards achieving.

- **Acquire as much knowledge as you can** - learn as much as you can about the firm you are joining in advance, whether this is information relating to their products and services, competition, clients, strategy, recent activity, or other helpful information. Carrying out extensive research into these areas will help you understand who your new employer is and their current circumstances **[see CHAPTER 6]**. When starting a new role at a new firm, your biggest challenge is your lack of understanding of your firm compared to your stakeholders and peers. When you have started in your role, you can further develop your knowledge in this area. In the meantime, obtain as much insight as readily available. Be sure to ask your new manager to send you any essential reading ahead of you starting - this also signals to them that you are proactive and keen to develop.

- **"Dot the i's and cross the t's"** - ensure you review and complete all the required documents and processes needed to start your new role. There is nothing more frustrating than beginning without a laptop; doing this stage is essential in helping the internal teams make sure your first day runs smoothly.

## Expert view
Katy Foster, Head of Business Development at Paul Hastings, based in Paris:

*"I recently joined Paul Hastings as Head of Business Development in Paris. Entering a new firm is such an exciting time. I remember feeling both very excited and scared. What if this was all a terrible mistake? I can assure you it's not, and in any case, I'm a strong believer in embracing failure. Joining a new firm is very challenging. Here are a few tips that I would recommend:*

*Before joining Paul Hastings, I utilised my professional network and gathered genuine internal feedback through social media platforms such as LinkedIn or peer groups, about my new firm.*

*I would also recommend that you meet as many people as possible when you join. Reach out to all your internal stakeholders and contact your peers to introduce yourself to, creating a platform for the years to come. First impressions matter, and they will follow you for the rest of your career at the firm.*

*I also believe that integration plays a significant part in the success of your new role. Onboarding can take two months to a year, depending on your position and responsibilities.*

*Keep showing up, keep showing your worth and delivering results, but most of all, keep learning."*

## ACCLIMATISE [Days 0 - 30]

- **Start as you mean to go on** - for the first month at your new firm, focus and invest your time building relationships and learning. Schedule as many as 30-minute face-to-face or virtual meetings with your team members, wider Marketing teams, peers, leadership, key internal stakeholders and other functions that will help you operate in your role. Seek to understand what each individual does in their role, who they are accountable to and most importantly, what they are focused on achieving. Asking lots of open-ended questions and building up your understanding in this way will ensure you quickly grasp the firm and the individuals within it that will help you succeed in your new role. [see PART THREE AND FOUR]

### In practice

Starting a new role is challenging, and you must develop new relationships and understand who everyone is and what they do. Considerable time and effort are required to thrive in your new role. Whether advising which experts to bring into your marketing initiative or seeking out others in the Marketing team who can work with you on completing a specific task, you need to have an internal network.

Moving to Eversheds Sutherland was slightly daunting due to the size of the firm globally and the different functions, teams and stakeholders I would need to get to know in my new role. But developing an understanding is critical to perform my international responsibilities, which is a priority area of my role. I needed to have relationships with stakeholders across the globe and have intimate knowledge across all functions as to who does what and who can help me most. To do this, I asked my line manager to firstly write out every key stakeholder I needed to "please". Then I focused on those in the Marketing team that could help me thrive in the role, e.g. pitch, design and anyone else helpful. Last but not least, I focused on other functions, e.g. research team, HR, finance specific contacts for HR issues and finance for marketing budget/expenses guidance. Then I went about building relationships with these individuals.

It is also helpful that you ask everyone, *"who else can you introduce me to that would be a useful contact for me to know?"*. Developing relationships is key to your learning about the firm. Your job is to listen, learn and ultimately synthesise all that you hear about, building an understanding of the significant issues and opportunities in your new role.

Within my first month at Eversheds, I had 200+ Skype calls. I would proactively schedule calls to develop my understanding of the firm, culture, and what most individuals did. It also allowed me to establish my reputation internally quickly, as being highly visible is vital when working with a broad group of stakeholders.

- **Be friendly and upbeat** - it sounds straightforward, but first impressions do count. Your peers and stakeholders are more likely to warm to you and help you settle in if you create a positive first impression as we all want to work with those we like. It sounds like common sense, but no matter how bad your day is going, *"how are you?"*, *"please"* and *"thank you"* go a long way.

- **Know your clients** - developing a comprehensive understanding of your clients is critical to performing in your role [see **CHAPTER 6**]. Building this understanding allows you to assess how to best engage with your target audience and segment it when planning future marketing initiatives you will be leading. Obtain internal information on your clients and what the firm does for each. Review any client feedback available, and if possible, try to get as much exposure as possible to your clients.

- **Infrastructure** - ensure you get important weekly or monthly meetings in your calendar. Add yourself to all the crucial internal Outlook contact groups to ensure you do not miss essential information or team requests. Check what colleagues in Marketing are on and which you should be on also.

- **Complete all of your training** - professional service firms are notorious for rigorous training that requires several hours of your time carrying out mandatory e-learning covering legal, bribery, IT and health & safety. Before leaping into the details of your new role, ensure you allocate as much time in the first week to complete most, if not all, of your required training. Once done, you can focus on the role at hand.

- **You're new here; ask questions** - make the most of this stage to ask as many questions so you can get a feel for the firm, culture, strategy, products, jargon and other valuable areas.

- **Organise accordingly** - we all have different ways to organise our calendars, emails, computer set-ups, apps, and specific equipment essential to do your role. Ensure you spend time setting this all up and working with IT / facilities to ensure you have the resources you need to perform in your position. If you are unfamiliar or new to the industry, seek out insight into how others organise themselves [see **CHAPTER 6**].

- **Connect and build awareness** - as discussed in the previous chapter, to begin developing your internal reputation, utilise LinkedIn by connecting with peers and stakeholders across the company. [see **CHAPTER 13**]

- **Assess the team (for line managers)** - If you are inheriting a team in your new role, begin by assessing and understanding their roles, clarifying what they do and how they allocate their working day towards their priorities and whether they are aligned to firm objectives. Seek to understand their aspirations, motivations, interests and ideas. Assess their strengths and weaknesses through reviewing their past performance reviews or obtaining feedback from peers and stakeholders. You can form your judgement, but these approaches are helpful for now.

- **Review the current position** - someone who was likely doing your role before or created a need for your job. You must review all previous activities and performances. Assess what each initiative sets out to achieve, its performance and critical lessons learnt - reviewing marketing plans or discussing with stakeholders is an excellent place to start. Learning from the mistakes and successes of others will help you avoid making the same mistakes and build on what has worked further in your new role.
- **Acclimatise to the culture [starting a role overseas]** - the industry's international nature allows you opportunities in your career to move internationally to seek new experiences [see Chapter 15].

## Expert view
Barbara Koenen-Geerdink, BD and Marketing Director at Al Tamimi & Co, based in Dubai:

*Starting a new job can be challenging on its own and even more so when you start a new job in a foreign country. Preparing for the big move, moving and finally also settling in will take time. Getting adjusted to your new way of living in a new country, especially if this involves learning about cultural differences and potentially also learning a new language, is not easy. Subsequently, your job will also require you to learn about the market in which the firm operates. The whole process can be overwhelming, but it is also exhilarating.*

*If you move overseas, you will likely encounter cultural differences, and you will have to adjust to the people you will work with, your new colleagues. You will need to make an effort to understand their values and what drives and motivates them. With cultural differences, undoubtedly, you will face some challenges. Approaching your colleagues, asking questions, and listening to them is excellent to understand their background. Also, ask your new colleagues simple questions like why they are doing what they are doing, and consequently, you will know what services the firm offers, who is doing what and who has specific responsibilities, and who the key stakeholders are. Always good to know. Showing a genuine interest in the people you work with will help you be perceived as interested and willing to learn. Also, ask your colleagues tips on dealing with cultural differences, how to best approach people, and generally understand the expectations of dealing with the people in the firm. Try not to make any assumptions or to be prejudiced but instead, keep an open mind and show respect.*

*Also really important for your success at your new firm in this new country is to understand the firm's markets. You will need to research to understand the dynamics of the markets, the key businesses, key players and understand how they carry out business generally as this may differ from jurisdiction to jurisdiction.*

*It is also helpful to know who your competitors are, using directories, benchmarking competitor data and speaking with industry experts, who know the market and country well. Make friends with people who can help you with relevant market intelligence and make sure to stay connected. As much as we advise our fee earners to network and connect with potential clients, take the same approach and network with both industry experts and your internal stakeholders.*

*You decided to work in a new country, by choice (one would hope at least) so also don't forget to enjoy the journey. Before moving to Dubai, I worked in Doha, Qatar, and before starting my career, I interned in New York and obtained a Master's Degree in business in Barcelona.*

*Learning about new cultures, religions and meeting new people is exciting and instantly adds to your life experience. Don't be shy to ask questions, show respect, adjust to local standards if required, and it will surely be a successful experience."*

## ESTABLISH: [Days 30-90]

- **Create credibility** - you have since completed your first month, and it will be essential to establish your reputation and credibility further across the firm and with VIP stakeholders. To do this, you should start your journey of becoming a go-to expert in one area of your role internally [see CHAPTER 13].

- **Identify your VIPs** - there is a structure and hierarchy for every firm, regardless of how informal or flat they claim to be. There will always be pockets of influence, authority, and power which are unlikely to be reflected accurately in any organisation structure chart you will come across. It is recommended you observe and create your stakeholder map during this stage [see CHAPTER 15].

- **Build your delivery team** - Identify and develop relationships with the teams and individuals you will need to get things done to achieve your objectives [see CHAPTER 10].

- **Formalise your Objectives** - ahead of you joining, you have already clarified the expectations from your manager as to what success looks like in your new role. Now is the time to agree and finalise what your objectives are. Work with your manager to track progress against these and send timely updates and reporting on successes. Ensure you carve out time each week to focus on these.

- **Focus on quick wins** - when starting a new role, you should assess everything objectively and identify where you can bring different insights from your previous firms and positions that will allow you to secure quick wins. Achieving this is the best way to establish credibility and build momentum that will set you up for future success at the firm. Your first month was your chance to understand the firm, whereas the following months are where you need to be generating tangible results.

- **Lead and empower others** - in the first month, you will have had many discussions with peers and stakeholders, where you will hear *"doing X would help the firm"*, so your response as a leader should be, *"what would it take for us to do X? What support do you need from me?"*, then asking a team member *"could you take on X?"*. Getting others to take ownership of ideas they have discovered is critical to achieving positive momentum and success. This also builds a good relationship with your team and others who previously didn't have someone like you to encourage their ideas and establish an open culture.

- **Pilot ideas and disruption** - having developed an understanding of the firm's strategy and past performance, now is the time to plan and implement marketing initiatives to achieve tangible results for the firm aligned to your objectives set by your manager. Look for ways to improve the firm, whether corporate culture, saving time and resources **[see CHAPTER 11]**.
- **Measure KPIs** - you must start developing a record of your achievements and performance. Setting clear KPIs for each initiative you work on and monitoring performance is a great way to demonstrate ROI back to your stakeholders **[see CHAPTER(S) 7 and 8]**.

## Expert view
Hannah Smith-Pickup, Clients and Industries Lead (North West) at Deloitte, based in Manchester:

*"Starting a new marketing leadership role in the middle of a pandemic was not something that I had envisioned, however when I started a new role at one of the 'Big 4' in 2020, it was something I had to face, rather suddenly. How would I develop relationships with my stakeholders and ensure I could disseminate the value I could bring when stuck at home? In my interview, I talked about the importance of communication, particularly around making the most of face-to-face contact when influencing and building those initial relationships, so I had to rethink my credibility. Therefore the value I would bring to the role. There were three things I focused on and continue to prioritise when I want to demonstrate my (and my wider team's) value to the business:*

*The power of listening: we all have ideas when we come to a new role, particularly around how we want to make changes in wanting to put our stamp on things - that's often the key to a successful interview. However, marketing practises have usually been well embedded in any professional services firm for many years, whether right or wrong. Changes can't be made overnight despite seeming evident to an outsider coming in. When I joined my new role. In developing my stakeholder relationships, I used the first few weeks to go through a consultation process, asking questions about the current market activity, what was working and what wasn't and what they would like to see scaling. I asked the questions, and I listened and listened some more. It allowed me to learn what made the practice tick and what marketing and BD meant to them and build trust with those stakeholders. It was all conducted virtually but having that 1-2-1 connection allowed me to establish some crucial relationships, particularly with members of the leadership team.*

*Planning and tangible objectives: the consultation process provided vital information needed for me to start building a strategic plan of delivery which in theory should appeal to all those I had met. I ensured the plan met the key stakeholders' needs (for the most part), and even when there were some conflicting ideas, I confirmed that the plan included at least one suggestion from each person.*

*In addition to the plan, I also set about creating some very tangible actions that I would focus on both short- and long-term. These were mainly for my stakeholders and close team - what could I achieve and provide value in both six months and 12 months. The critical thing here was not to over-promise too much - we can all get carried away with focusing on taking on too many things and trying to fix everything in new roles.*

*Strategic communication: so we had the plan, the priorities, and we were working on some significant initiatives, but how would the various groups know what we were doing, mainly as we couldn't rely on those office 'watercooler' conversations, plus my practice was upwards of 800 people. It was essential to identify the key groups I had to make my mark and convey my value: the leadership team, the partner and director groups and the broader practice. What were the regular meetings that I could join? Both small and larger sessions. In doing this, I ensured the Marketing team's activities, capabilities and credibility by requesting regular slots at those meetings and tapping into any practice-wide communication channels. I created a quarterly market impact report which regularly demonstrated our activities, the strength of the team and, therefore, the value we were bringing around client development and amplifying our voice into the market. And where appropriate, I was able to call out individual team members' activities in demonstrating their specific value. As such, I was able to amplify and build our team's brand identity to be all about added value."*

## BEYOND [Days 90+]

- **Seek feedback** - consider obtaining formal feedback from your line manager, peers, and key stakeholders. Ask them to focus on what is working well and areas to improve - helping you gauge the impact you are making and where to improve when starting a new role [see CHAPTER(S) 9,13,14].
- **Talent management** - if you manage a team, you will have had the opportunity to assess whether you have the right people to support the firm strategy. If not, you will have to make changes through developing existing talent, reconfiguring your team, or bringing in external talent.It is important you have the right team to support you to perform and meet your objectives.
- **Develop yourself** - identify career development resources and internal training opportunities to develop your technical skills, soft skills and learning gaps. Speak to your internal learning & development team, identify external providers to help you grow in these areas, and courses. [see CHAPTER 17].
- **Start planning for the future** - building off the quick wins and early results you have achieved in your role will give you the confidence and momentum to focus on your long-term objectives and ambitions in your new position. Review your objectives set by your manager and what are the following steps to develop in your role [see CHAPTER 18].

**Key points to remember**

1.  Before starting your new role, you should prepare as much as possible. When you officially start, follow the above 90-day plan to ensure you acclimatise, establish yourself and then consider how you continue to develop beyond this.

2.  It would help if you built up as much of an understanding of your new firm as quickly as possible to thrive in your new role. Schedule introductory meetings with key stakeholders and ask them, "who else can you introduce me to that would be a useful contact for me to know?".

3.  Once you have completed your first month, you must establish your reputation and credibility across the firm and with key stakeholders. To do this, you should start your journey of becoming a go-to expert in one area of your role internally.

4.  Start planning for the future by building off the quick wins and early results you have achieved in your role; this will give you the confidence and momentum to focus on your long-term objectives and ambitions in your new role. Review the objectives set by your manager and the following steps to develop in your position.

# 3

# Preparing for promotion

*"Some people want it to happen, some wish it would happen,
others make it happen"*
*—Michael Jordan*

It is more difficult to advance your career in your current firm than pursue career opportunities externally. This is because you might be doing your job well, but there is no guarantee that your efforts will lead to a promotion. Moreover, the promotion process is often unclear and challenging. You need to do several key things well to succeed in your role to get promoted.

## Clearly define the next career step

It is often unclear what the next step is and when the next promotion is coming in your career. Proactive career planning is essential to help you identify the next steps in your career [see **CHAPTER 16**].

Before you pursue your next career step and focus your efforts on being promoted into this role, you should develop a thorough understanding of the skills required and the specific responsibilities for the position, and this will most importantly clarify if this is a role you want to do for in your career.

Once you have identified the next step, you must seek out these individuals within your firm and industry who hold these positions to learn from them. If you work closely with them already, you may well be learning from them. A mentorship or the opportunity to shadow them on initiatives you are working closely together are further ways to build on this and get a more in-depth understanding of what it takes to perform and reach this role.

Knowing the role's responsibilities will also help you understand the next step and what you need to do to prepare for the position should it present itself in the future.

You may conclude that the next step in your career is a position that doesn't exist at your firm, so it is vital to research your competitors, talk to recruiters, and seek out individuals in these roles in the industry. Then, using this information in your appraisal, you can explain to your manager why such a role is needed and why you are best qualified for the position.

## Seeking out promotion opportunities in your firm

It is possible to get promoted when your peers and the marketing leadership team recognise and consider you the only viable candidate who can progress and perform in the role; this often occurs where you might be filling in for a role on an interim basis. As for senior positions, several internal candidates will frequently apply for a job that will allow them to advance their careers to the next level. If you are successful in your approach, your relationship with these individuals would be affected, and you would need to rebuild it.

You are typically not told that internal promotions are often within your reach. Often they can be influenced by external factors out of your control, e.g. team departures. Some elements are within your control, such as consistently demonstrating to key stakeholders that you are someone the firm should invest in developing and progressing your career within the firm. Furthermore, there are instances where you can identify a clear gap you can fill and build a business case for why a new senior position needs creating. Often harder to achieve because marketing headcounts are often tight, and additional budgets might not be available during the current financial year.

Communicating your desire for a specific promotion to your manager as part of your appraisal process [see CHAPTER 18]. Establish that you want a promotion, and they may respond favourably by defining what you need to do.

It is crucial to position yourself for promotional opportunities; this is done by consistently demonstrating your desire and ability to solve problems, solidifying your value to the firm and how you can contribute to the firm's performance as a whole.

It can be challenging to identify where future career opportunities are available in your firm unless you regularly discuss your career advancement in your appraisal with your manager. Not doing this means you can often be working hard based on the hope of being promoted.

Before being considered for promotion, the firm and your manager will look for certain things from you. Such as taking on key initiatives on your own, consistently receiving positive feedback from senior stakeholders, helping to raise others' performance, and making life easier for your manager.

When your manager or the marketing leadership team signals to you that there is an opportunity for you to advance your career to the next level, you can begin to turn your attention and focus on how you obtain this promotion.

- Take time to review and assess your business case, examples of how you have added value to the firm, improved the team and received feedback from stakeholders.
- Identify how your experience and skills can contribute to the role and identify weaknesses in your expertise that need to be

developed to succeed. It is important you really assess which areas you need to develop in.

- Research the market outside the firm to learn about typical advancement opportunities and benchmark your salary beyond the role within the firm.
- Explain how you will contribute to the firm when promoted.

Getting such an opportunity means preparing in advance to increase your chances of a successful promotion, which will also serve you well in your promotion application and interviews, when the time comes:

## Expert view   Lucy Canning, Head of Marketing & Business Development at Grant Thornton, based in London:

*"In the earlier stages of my career, whilst I always had active roles, I would often put myself forward to work on other projects that increase my exposure t a wide team I regularly asked if I could provide an extra pair of hands for large scale marketing initiatives and campaigns to volunteer myself to support the annual marketing planning process. It meant I had a lot on my plate, but in doing this, I built up new skills, developed relationships with senior stakeholders, learned from them, and ultimately built my profile.*

*I always looked to experiment with new tools, new approaches, which again built up my experience and exposure. Taking this proactive approach and being genuinely interested in supporting the bigger picture and the broader ecosystem (and not just what was on my job description) made my role(s) more exciting and challenging.*

*But when I look back, doing these things was why I was in strong positions for promotions and selection for more senior roles.*

*I was inadvertently developing the credentials, the relationships, and the perception of myself that to some extent spoke for itself."*

## Imposter syndrome and overconfidence

There are also instances when more senior roles in the business might become available to you that you might not have considered being within your grasp for several reasons, whether this is lack of seniority, skillset gaps, or another reason. Part of this stems from imposter syndrome, a collection of feelings of inadequacy that persist despite evident success. If left unchecked, it can undermine your confidence, performance and motivation.

According to Wharton researcher Basima Tewfik, her research found, interestingly, that having imposter thoughts improves interpersonal performance at work and can be used as a motivator to perform in a senior role.

In contrast to this, like many, perhaps you overestimate yourself (this is called the Dunning- Kruger effect), which leads to you becoming overconfident in your belief in your abilities and suitability for promotional opportunities. If you are not careful, your approach can sabotage your career prospects by being considered entitled. Even worse, when you are unsuccessful in achieving a promotion, it can be a stark reality check and create future self-doubt.

## Understand the process

Therefore the key to preparing for promotion is to consider and be aware of the process in which professional service firms approach promotion opportunities. Across firms, the process will vary significantly. For example, is your firm committed to reviewing internal candidates before going to market for positions? If so, this will limit your competition for senior roles.

Develop an understanding of the administrative and various hurdles you need to jump through, whether an interview with a committee, a formal report stating the business case or an interim trial basis. Being clear on what is required when the opportunity presents itself is important because often, the you.

When a promotion becomes available, most firms run promotions on cycles such as the end of the financial year or when several of the team have recently left the firm, allowing the additional budget to support creating a new position. You must be clear on the process to ensure you do not spend the next six months waiting for the next budgetary cycle before a promotion is possible and instead you can be promoted as timely as possible

## Importance of stakeholders and "career champions"

You could be the hardest worker and most talented professional in your firm. Still, if no one knows this or can share this with the broader business, but most importantly, the key decision-makers that are leading promotion opportunities in your firm, then it will be all for nothing.

I want you to picture the marketing leadership team at your firm discussing promotional candidates for a vacant senior role. Who in that group is most likely to champion you for such a role? What senior stakeholders across the business regularly "sing your praises" to the marketing leadership? Do HR, Finance, and other functions know you?

We cover internal stakeholder management in detail later in the book [see CHAPTER 4]. Still, it is essential to stress the role your internal stakeholders play in contributing to whether you are put forward for promotion and selected to advance your career into senior positions in your firm.

As discussed previously, you must share your intentions with your line manager to pursue opportunities internally. Communicate your intentions during your appraisal or scheduling time to discuss [see CHAPTER 18]. Also, this is an excellent way to gauge your development and whether your line manager perceives you to be ready for the promotion and whether they are prepared to help your cause. If so, they will be someone that will be key to the process when asked for your feedback as part of your application. By sharing your intention with them, you also avoid the risk of being overlooked for such a position, as you had not communicated it was of interest internally.

Focusing solely on your line manager is an area most of us do well, but you need to be aware that their input into the promotion process is a part of the decision-making process of whether or not to promote you, not the final decision.

If you are working a logical step above you, you likely know the key stakeholders, and they probably have a perception of your ability and whether you can move up into the senior position. Of course, if this is all positive, your rise will be more straightforward to the reverse if they do not see you stepping up. The key to reversing this is to demonstrate and perform above their current expectations by focusing on supporting those stakeholders to help them reach their objectives, show consistent results in your role on complex initiatives that would often be the responsibility of the senior position.

Suppose you are internally preparing for a promotion opportunity outside your current focus in a different team. It will be more challenging to develop new relationships with the key stakeholders. This will require you to be proactive and seek out broad initiatives that allow you to work directly with these stakeholders.

In terms of your manager and the leadership team in Marketing, you must seek out and volunteer to handle the most complex or business-critical initiatives that will help the firm work towards its objectives or lead to robust ROI. Suppose your manager has line management responsibilities for several individuals. In that case, it is vital that you track your activity and results and then present these back to them at your appraisal [see CHAPTER 18]. These actions will signal to them that you deserve investment and career advancement opportunities at the firm. Also, the more you can work closely with your manager to help them progress their objectives, the more they will become a champion for you, which will be covered in more detail later on in the book.

The promotion process often involves multiple other functions outside of Marketing that help pass through approval for a promotion or form part of the decision-making committee as to whether you get promoted or not. It is essential to understand the key stakeholders in these functions, develop a relationship with them, and remain visible in your role.

Another key tactical move to make promotion and have already established a strong relationship with one of the critical stakeholders in that group is to utilise this champion to further your promotional push.

Discuss with them that you have applied for the opportunity to. They may be willing to support your promotion efforts, if you could build trust with these stakeholders such as emailing your line manager or the CMO; it helps your cause mainly when the CMO sees the main stakeholder is advocating for you to take on this role. If you do not have a relationship with the stakeholder for an internal promotion, you will have to invest your time and take on specific projects to put yourself on their radar.

## Keep focused

When you are in the process of being promoted, it is likely that other opportunities internally and externally may become available. It can be far easier to move externally or be tempted in the short term to switch your focus to another senior role internally. Avoid focusing on short term gains: this could lead to you moving the prospect or interest into a position you do not initially want and will reset all the hard work you have invested towards your promotion.

## Recognise your competitive advantage over external candidates

Often overlooked, you must recognise your value proposition compared to external candidates. Consider the benefits you would bring to a specific role compared to external candidates, examples include:

- understanding of the firmwide strategy and products/services;
- proven track record of working in the firm and performing in the structure/culture;
- relationships with key stakeholders;
- peer relationships across the Marketing team;
- cost-effective compared to recruitment costs and higher salary package required for external candidate search;
- able to start in a new role, sooner than those with a long notice period.

Being aware of these benefits is vital for your application and internal interviews. Review these to provide you with added confidence when your skills and experience might be lacking compared to the requirements of a senior role.

## Setting yourself up for success after being promoted

Following your promotion success, you must prepare yourself for your new role. Likely, your transition into your new position will not be instantaneous with an internal promotion unless you're already doing this role in an interim or non-formal capacity.

If, instead, you are moving to a new role, there will be much change, which will require you to refocus your priorities, acquire knowledge and build relationships with stakeholders. Before being promoted to your new position officially, it is critical that you:

- **Become clear on your future priorities and tasks** - you can do this by shadowing someone in the current role if at the firm still or reviewing the handover notes and the job specification if one is available.
- **Acquire as much knowledge required to operate in your new role** - research to understand the specific technical skills needed and learning; for example, if you move into a sector-focused position, you must understand the sector.

- **Refocus your stakeholders** - it is crucial that you first communicate such a change to your existing stakeholders when they have changed. If not done, they will probably consider you in your current role and responsible for delivering output aligned to their objectives. Managing their expectations is even more critical where the firm has not found a replacement for your role yet.
- **Assess the situation** - you must gain knowledge and insight into previous initiatives and the results when moving into the new role. Focus on understanding the strategy and stakeholder dynamics around which initiatives are sacred by internal and external clients. If you are stepping into a position with a team, ensure you learn from them and find out what they think your priorities should be that previously did not get addressed by your predecessor.

The next point is to be clear on the role's responsibilities and understand the strategy, core initiatives, market position and other strategic information. Focus on the learning side of your role in the first instance and try not to disrupt ongoing marketing initiatives and the strategy in place too quickly at risk of stopping those initiatives that are working. It is also imperative that you get the perspective of any of your team. With you becoming their line manager, they will be assessing and uncertain of their career future under your new leadership. How you work with them will be critical, so understanding their ambitions and ideas for change that the previous leadership culture might have suppressed.

As you transition from one role to another, your stakeholders are likely to have also changed, so you must align your time and energy towards developing a trusting relationship with these stakeholders and asking what has been working, what has not, what they would like to see changed, and what they expect of you. Not only is this crucial to building relationships, but it will also provide you with a valuable overview of your new role, the existing strategy and help you determine what quick wins you can achieve in your position. Not just for you but for those that championed the firm's investment and commitment in backing your promotion, you must settle in quickly and begin to show results soon.

Adapting your approach and communication style is essential when promoted into a senior role. As you transition into your new position, you must assess your professional internal brand to consider how you want to be perceived internally and act accordingly. Your relationship with other team members and those in your team may have to be reset if you're now responsible for managing them. However, this does not mean you cannot have a good working relationship; it is about making sure they understand your new role and how your relationship at work needs to change in terms of what you expect from them and how they should operate around you.

The whole experience will benefit your career no matter how successful your promotion efforts are. Well done if you get the promotion, your career just advanced. Don't be downhearted if someone else gets the role instead of you. As part of your career progression journey, you will be giving a great impression of yourself to management, and there will be several other opportunities in the future.

### In practice

The above steps have been implemented several times in my career when I've successfully been through the promotion process. Most recently in my career, after joining Eversheds Sutherland as a business development manager, my manager left after a few months. As a result, I was now accountable for challenging responsibilities I would have not previously encountered in my position.

As a result of my career, I did not envision myself as a senior manager when my manager left. Since I had been at the firm for a short period and was busy covering the increased workload, I did not expect to take on such a role.

I dispelled some of my earlier doubts after several months of demonstrating my ability to handle the responsibilities of the senior manager role, developing solid relationships with key stakeholders, and delivering several key initiatives that helped grow the firm in the sector significantly. As a new hire, I learned about the firm quickly, built stakeholder relationships, and learned and executed the sector's strategy. After learning much in such a short period, I quickly grasped my responsibilities, later stepping up my efforts to spend more time with stakeholders and focusing on what had worked in the past and at the same time stopping what had not.

Now I was responsible for leading the direction for EMEA, and I had to show that I could do such a role and fail fast and learn on the job with the added pressure of having this responsibility. Throughout many months, I demonstrated to my stakeholders that I was performing well. The marketing leadership team trusted me to handle the role in an interim capacity, during this period they sought no recruitment for the senior manager role.

Internal promotions can be complex; for instance, I managed the senior management role for over a year, but to get promoted, I had to develop my internal champions in the marketing leadership team and expand my stakeholder base in the sector. It was important that I regularly mentioned my interest in the role and being promoted in my appraisals. Understanding your firm's process, being resilient, and realising it can take a while for budget approvals, processes, sign-offs, and other steps. I got promoted at a difficult time when COVID-19 was constantly disrupting the industry, and when the budget heavily impacted my promotion process, I learned these lessons the hard way. It's important to remember that you can perform an internal role on an interim basis. Still, unless you persist and are proactive in pushing the process forward, you will have difficulty navigating the internal hurdles needed to achieve promotion.

## Gather feedback on performance and adapt accordingly

As soon as you are promoted into a role, whether it is an interim role or a new role within the team, you must regularly gather feedback. Not only as part of your appraisal but also as a continual process, mainly as you work with your new stakeholders. Each stakeholder has a different way of doing things, and you must align your expectations in respect of what they expect from you in your new role. Get specific feedback on your output, how they want you to communicate with them, what support they will appreciate.

When stepping up into a vacant role, where your predecessor either left the firm or moved internally, this step can be particularly beneficial if they have set positive expectations about what a person in your role can and should contribute, as stakeholders will likely compare you to them. If this person is still in the firm, I recommend spending as much time with them to understand what they did and what changes they always wanted to make but never had the time or support to implement.

In a newly created role, your stakeholders' expectations of you will be limited, which means you can craft your own expectations for the role:.

## Don't be complacent

When promoted, you are thrust into the spotlight by your peers and the marketing leadership team. They have invested in you and trusted you with greater responsibility to drive further growth at the firm following your promotion. Suppose your performance levels and results are not maintained to a similar level as performing at prior to your promotion. In that case, those internally might form the perception that you are short-term focused, who might lead to you being and might become overlooked for future promotion opportunities internally being.

Working towards a promotion can provide you with the added motivation to develop peak performance levels and hone your focus on achieving your objectives. However, upon your successful promotion, you find yourself faced with added responsibilities and expectations by the firm; it can be different to maintain these performance levels, mainly when there is no near-term prospect of career advancement.

It is crucial not to lose your determination and effort following your successful promotion. Because the promotion process can be complex and challenging, it can be challenging to maintain the same level of energy and determination that you previously demonstrated as part of the promotion process. While the positive perceptions you build and the trust you develop with specific stakeholders will last long after your promotion, you must maintain a consistently high level of work output and results. [see **CHAPTER 10**]

---

### ▶ Key points to remember

1. It is often unclear what the next step is and when the next promotion is coming in your career. A proactive career plan will help you identify your next career steps.

2. It is essential to communicate your manager's desire for a specific promotion. When you let them know you wish to be promoted, they may respond positively by pointing out what you need to do.

3. You need to understand the administrative and various hurdles you must overcome, such as an interview with a committee, a formal report stating the business case, or an interim trial basis.

4. You could be the most talented and hardworking professional in your firm. However, nothing will be accomplished if no one knows about this or can share it with the broader business. Most importantly, the key decision-makers driving promotion opportunities in your company.

---

# 4

# Climbing to the top

*"Only those who will risk going too far can possibly find out how far one can go"*
*—T. S. Eliot*

## Overview of the current climate

The CMO position is still relatively new within the professional services industry, and it is becoming more common for firms to have marketing representation on their board. Reuters reported in 2021 that at least 20 Am Law 200 firms brought on new chief marketing officers during the year. which is a testament to the elevation of this role in the sector,

The study noted that most companies (63%) promoted internal candidates to open CMO positions in 2020 rather than hiring externally, which increased to 84% among first-time CMOs.

According to the "AM Law 200 Marketing Leader Snapshot", current CMO tenures range from as little as five months up to twenty-nine+ years. Looking more broadly outside of just professional services, the average tenure for CMOs fell to 40 months in 2020, the shortest it has been since 2009, according to new research from leadership advisory firm Spencer Stuart.

This information highlights how professional services firms and how the rise in marketing talent into leadership positions shows positive progress. At the same time, it is worth remaining cautious as the tenure of CMOs continues to decline, therefore highlighting the importance of being prepared to walk into these positions and perform effectively.

## Expert view

Matthew Gardner, Director at Ambition, based in London:

*"Arguably, it's never been a better time to be a leader within a Marketing department in a professional services firm. The last couple of years has highlighted the growing importance of Marketing and the direct impact they have on the success of a firm, particularly around critical matters e.g. winning new business and retaining existing clients. This means leaders are now sitting at the board level within firms and have real influence over the strategic direction of those organisations.*

*In my role, my core focus is on C-suite and leadership positions in Marketing for professional services firms throughout the UK and internationally. I regularly work with senior partners and Chief People Officers to understand what they require in these positions now and in the future. If you are looking to take that next step in your career to a leadership level, here are a few points I think are critical for you achieving that step successfully in the future:*

- **Having clarity on why you want to be a BD Director or CMO** - *one of the consequences of taking on a leadership level role is that it can often take you further away from what you are passionate about most. Particularly in larger firms, your position becomes far more about people management, whether managing a large department (quite often across multi-jurisdictions) or managing lots of layers of stakeholders within a firm.*

   *Of course, not every CMO or Director role is the same. Every firm will have different approaches to their growth and what they expect from you as their leader regarding client attraction, brand refreshes, digitisation, people management, and other responsibilities. Therefore, you must clarify your strengths, passions, and expectations when moving into these roles. If there isn't good alignment, it won't work.*

- **Demonstrating commerciality -** *in line with more leaders having a seat at the table, there is a greater expectation of you demonstrating your commercial awareness. An essential skill at all levels, particularly when trying to influence a partnership, is to demonstrate the commercial benefit with your ideas and understand the wider firm (not just within Marketing) and the external market. You can hone these skills by spending more time with other departments to understand the business challenges and opportunities. Furthermore, one of the best ways to build your reputation internally and externally, so you can step into Director levels roles, is to showcase as many specific examples as possible of you bringing direct commercial benefit to your firm.*

- **Focus on personal branding, networking and career sponsors** *- your brand can play a big part in landing your dream job either in your current firm or at another firm in the industry. How you're perceived internally in your current firm or the market is fundamental, and this is an area I see many professionals overlook.*

  *There is plenty of material and tools to improve your brand, but I recommend attending as many relevant networking events as possible. If you're trying to take the step up in seniority, try to get in the room with other Directors and CMO's so you start networking at the right level and show you "belong". The market is tiny, and a few positive interactions can do wonders to elevate your brand.*

  *Furthermore, being part of networking groups or roundtables can be a great way to generate new ideas or use a sounding board which can be valuable in leadership roles when the buck stops with you. Given that the function continues to evolve, I would also recommend attending events outside the sector to gain best practice and, where appropriate, bring fresh ideas into your firm.*

  *To take this a step further, I would recommend identifying a senior mentor or sponsor within a firm that can help your personal development and help you open doors within other firms.*

- **Keeping up with evolving skills and trends whilst remaining authentic to your strengths** *- I am seeing an increased interest in* *digital and data from Managing Partners in professional services firms, demanding their CMO is at the forefront of driving client innovation and change. Therefore it is essential as a leader you display these traits and experiences.*

*However, each firm will be at different stages of evolution, and you must understand where your current or prospective firm is in terms of its change curve. If your strength is client development, for example, several firms currently have that as a strategic focus, it is again best to align your strengths with that of a firm when moving roles. Over time you will need to continue to upskill and evolve these skill sets, but this can be bridged with external learning and hiring great people around you."*

## What does a CMO do, and what skills are required?

According to Gartner, a simplified definition of a chief marketing officer (CMO) is "the corporate executive responsible for an organisation's marketing activities. The CMO's primary responsibility is to generate revenue by increasing sales through:

- Brand management
- Marketing communications
- Market research
- Product marketing
- Distribution channel management
- Pricing
- Customer service"

The role of a CMO in professional service firms has evolved dramatically and taken on increasing importance as firms adapt to globalisation, define their markets, and implement a go-to-market strategy to remain competitive. Not only is the CMO viewed as a business partner with the firm's advisors in defining and communicating a firm's brand, but a growing number of CMOs are charged with helping the firm secure and expand client relationships. And today's marketing leader has to recruit, retain and develop a cohesive and often geographically dispersed Marketing team.

What is clear from the above list is the importance of developing a broad understanding of the different technical areas of a CMO role. In doing so, you can advise the firm and your team on the strategic direction.

## Expert view

Sadie Baron, Chief Marketing Officer at Reed Smith and LMA Europe 2022 President, based in London. Sadie wrote the following for Totum Partners:

*"I often rally against the trend of specialising too soon: 'people get pigeon-holed too early. I look at marketers in the early years of their careers, and all they do is BD'.*

*I held various roles throughout my career. I rolled out the CRM system at Eversheds and got involved in data that I didn't think I'd like but loved. I looked after the corporate, commercial, and real estate practises and the London office. But my success also taught me a significant lesson that I have taken into my attitude to recruitment. 'You don't have to love the law or have a burning passion for it. It's about the right attitude. I will take people from FMCG or any other sector to demonstrate a love for marketing and BD, not necessarily the sector. I can train the other stuff, but I can't train the attitude.'*

*I also learned some other critical lessons along the way. After Eversheds, for instance, I spent a short time with PwC in the forensics department. Not a promotion - the friendly partners and the powerful brand won me over (and the opportunity to get some broader professional services experience). But it was an important step to gain the right tools for longer-term success. 'Don't be afraid of making lateral moves. I am CMO because I genuinely have BD, marketing, and CRM, and I understand data and other technical areas that are crucial to the role. I'm well versed in making* decisions and understanding the dynamics of what goes on and what's needed."

To be a successful CMO, you must be valued for your marketing expertise and the strategic perspective to the role. Even those at the CMO level can sometimes find themselves isolated at one end of the business, too far from the core processes. Most successful CMOs are considered experts in brand building, brand equity, and consumer insight, capable of mobilising a Marketing department. It is crucial; not to be seen as a marketing expert but as a potential leader capable of operating in the C-suite to be considered for the CMO position.

## Expert view

Jeff Berardi, Partner at legal advisory firm Baretz+Brunelle and former CMO at K&L Gates, based in Boston:

"Many marketing professionals are planning their next career move in the industry and are considering what they need to do to make it happen. Some have a long-term vision and the bold ambition of one day becoming a chief marketing officer (CMO) at a major professional services firm.

But the road to the top isn't always clear, and you may wonder what it truly takes to become a CMO. Reflecting on my elevation into the position, I'd like to share some practical guidance as you prepare for a potential rise to the top."

### Making the step up to a CMO position

I spent 13 years as CMO of K&L Gates, managing a team of approximately 100 people within the Marketing function. In this role, I was responsible for leading the global marketing, business development and sales activities for one of the largest corporate law firms in the world, with more than 40 offices located across five continents.

Before being appointed CMO in 2006, I didn't have any senior-level experience on the job. That said, I had been at the firm for a couple of *years in a mid-level manager role, where I had built strong relationships with influential partners and administrative professionals.*

*When the CMO position became available, I did not initially consider myself in contention for this high-level position. Instead, there was a director role that had become vacant at around the same time, and I felt like the typical trajectory would be to move up into that next level before being allowed to be considered as CMO.*

*Fortuitously, I had a supportive network of people - within and outside the firm - who suggested that I apply for the open CMO role. I'm honestly not sure if I would have had the confidence to throw my hat in the ring for this position if others had not prompted me to do so, and I'm very grateful to those who believed in me even before I had any experience; in the role.*

*After an initial meeting with the firm's global managing partner, Peter Kalis, I underwent a rigorous vetting process with internal and external candidates. That stage lasted a month or two. I oversaw several significant firm projects, which allowed me to work hard and prove myself to the global managing partner and others involved in the decision-making.*

*Those weeks were intense, but they enabled me to build up trust and rapport with Pete and others that I hadn't had a chance to get to know previously. There were some challenging days and nights, but I believe they were critical to being considered as a viable candidate for the CMO role."*

*Eventually, I was offered the role of Acting CMO, which I held for approximately six months before being elevated into the full CMO position.*

### Challenges of being promoted into a new challenging role

*When appointed into a senior position, a significant challenge was overseeing team members formerly at the same level as you. Some of your team will be okay with this, and others may not be, particularly those who thought they should have the role. So do expect to encounter some resistance in your new role.*

*An effective learning process for the early years in my role as CMO, I found it essential to establish some boundaries with the team. Although*

*I still maintained strong personal relationships with individuals, I ensured that they understood the objectives and expectations in their roles. I also learned the importance of empowering the team and not micromanaging individuals. This is particularly true for the more senior team members, as those were people that I wanted to develop trust quickly.*

*I had to get to grips with challenging parts of the new role, such as handling those not flourishing in their roles. I had to make some changes within the team that not everyone agreed with, so it was not always easy or utterly smooth sailing.*

*I often sought out those in the team that were most adaptable and who bought into the strategic direction. Somewhat not surprisingly, those individuals often stayed at the firm the longest and rose in the team.*

*A fundamental change that was also going on that changed the dynamic of my role was the merger of Kirkpatrick & Lockhart Nicholson Graham with Preston Gates in 2007 to form K&L Gates. Not only doubling headcount within the Marketing team but also allowed me to reimagine and restructure the department based on a long-term rather than short-term vision.*

*I wasn't wedded to the existing structure of the Marketing team since I was new to the CMO role and was already considering making changes based on how best to support the firm's current and future goals. The 2007 merger with Preston Gates & Ellis enabled me to see the team with a fresh set of eyes, and I was able to make more dramatic organisational changes than when I first became CMO in 2006."*

**Thriving and lessons learned in the role**

- ***Be authentic to yourself*** - *I did not initially have any direct experience in a senior-level role when I landed the interim CMO position and later the CMO position. As I entered these roles, I felt like I had to prove to the Marketing team and wider stakeholders that I could do this role. Looking back on those early days in the position, I probably was at times too autocratic in how I wanted others around me to act in a certain way, perhaps feeling that they needed to comply with my leadership. With the benefit of hindsight, I have since found it more effective to create* *a collaborative culture where my team knows they must work hard to perform at a high level, but they are motivated and challenged to do their best work. Focus on giving people an opportunity to make mistakes without being so hard on them.*

- **The team is crucial to your success –** *I always had great people supporting me, and I tried to give them the ability to lead their teams in the right way. I didn't feel like I needed to tell them how to do their job. I wanted to find intelligent and capable people that I could provide with the direction to thrive. I found much success in building a culture where the team members could speak up and say, "Hey Jeff, I wonder if we tried a different approach?" At the same time, it is essential to develop loyal team members that can follow directions without poking holes at everything.*

- **In global roles, your stakeholders are everywhere** *- as CMO for the entire firm, I had members of the Management Committee (regional managing partners, practice area leaders, other Chiefs.) based worldwide. They looked to me for anything related to marketing and business development, as I was responsible for my team and its activities regardless of location. It was important that my internal stakeholders felt supported, knowing that specific initiatives were moving forward. I maintained close communication so that partners and other key stakeholders could reach out to me whenever and wherever needed. I invested the time making trips worldwide and getting to know these stakeholders personally. If I could not visit those locations and get to know partners in various offices, I honestly don't think I would have succeeded. Now you can do some of it by Zoom, but it doesn't have the same impact as making an effort to be visible with these stakeholders and enjoy a meal or several in-person discussions with them.*

- **Don't be afraid to seek out critical feedback** *- being an outlet for these stakeholders is incredibly important, as it provides an opportunity for them to share feedback - good and bad. Do not be afraid to hear the bad stuff; this is what you want as you can hopefully address it. It can be something as simple as market collateral in the lobby of an* *overseas office. In other cases, it isn't something that you can quickly fix, but you may provide some important context for why the firm has chosen to proceed in a particular way. Which can often alleviate the issues felt at the local level.*

*I viewed it as anything to do with marketing, and BD was on my shoulders, and it was ultimately my responsibility. That meant that I would try to find some solution to whatever issue people faced. Not so much pointing fingers like, this team member isn't doing their job well, but more like "we're not addressing certain stakeholder needs right here, how can we fix this?" It is essential to ensure you do not jump to conclusions on feedback. Instead, it's often better to objectively investigate the root issue that needs addressing, whether miscommunication or expectations are not aligned.*

- **Set processes and rules to govern and empower your team** – *as CMO, it is beneficial to establish what your team can and cannot do. Allow the team to provide a unified set of messages to stakeholders asking for something the firm should not reasonably support. Make sure that you get buy-in and support from the top so that when you or your team does push back, it is a "firm decision" rather than simply a "Marketing department decision." To avoid engaging in specific marketing opportunities that are not beneficial for the firm, establish policies that will enable you to manage stakeholders and focus the firm in the right direction. Frequently, I wasn't just saying to one of my managers or directors, "go tell this partner we're not going to do it." It was more along the lines of "let's look into this a bit more, can we assess the pros and cons with the stakeholders", or we would work directly with the practice area leader or head of that office to say, "Here's what we assessed. Here's another approach that we could take. Do you agree with and support that direction?"*

- **Utilise data and connect it to revenue generation –** *Having access to data and using this information is critical in your role to demonstrate a connection between the Marketing team's output and the various benefits it is bringing to the firm. An analytical approach also works well with senior stakeholders who often respond better to numbers* *and data than your experience or instincts. Particularly in the role of a CMO, revenue generation is something that the firm is expecting from you - the more you can connect the initiatives and activities that you and your team are pursuing (inclusive of marketing communications, business development, and other efforts) with measurable revenue generation, the more successful you'll be."*

## Adding value as an integral member of your firm's leadership team

CMOs find themselves exerting more influence over strategy as the role of marketing continues to evolve, taking on a more significant leadership and responsibility for growth. Careful thought needs to go into your career planning. If you wish to become a CMO, you must grasp every opportunity to step out of your comfort zone and expose yourself to situations and challenges that will help prepare you for a C-suite leadership role.

The pressures to demonstrate outcomes and return on investment are immense when operating in a CMO position. Marketing has always struggled with measuring the impact of their activities, and it is now more vital for them to do so [see **CHAPTER 8**]. Given the intelligent control of all costs in companies today, marketing budgets, in general, are tightening. And marketing spending is always on the radar of the chief financial officer. To be a genuinely strategic CMO, one must instil a firmwide mindset of considering metrics not just as a barometer or an output but as a critical input for decision-making.

Digital marketing provides powerful new tools and metrics to measure the impact and effectiveness of your firm's marketing efforts. The more successfully you can demonstrate a direct link between spending and revenues in your role, the tremendous success you will have in the boardroom. There remain elements of the position, such as measuring the precise impact of digital marketing and social media activities on fee generation and the bottom line for your firm, which created immediate pressure on CMOs to cut what is not, resulting in immediate ROI.

**Expert view**  Richard Grove, former Global Chief Marketing & Communications Officer at Allen & Overy, which he held for 14 years, as a member of the leadership team and Global Executive Committee, based in London:

*"Strong and successful leadership of a firm Marketing and BD function is an art, and with it can only be partially learned - the fundamentals come from the individual's character and match the firm's culture.*

*Recruitment consultants and senior partners can tick as many boxes as they like for CMO candidates' professional marketing and BD skillsets. Still, it will count for nothing if the individual does not empathise with how to succeed in a partnership and has a natural flair for leadership.*

*A law firm CMO's typical life expectancy is scarily short. That is often because CMO's will not understand that their success is measured in terms of the trust and respect of the partners and the BD team - and it has to be both. Trust and respect are earned and usually requires 'authentic' leadership, and authenticity requires some vulnerability, which doesn't come naturally to some senior people focussed on status.*

*Probably the single biggest impediment to the success of a CMO in a law firm is ego. Good marketing and salespeople are instinctively empathetic and attuned to influencing people - that's at the core of their job for the external target audiences. But it's essential for the internal audiences too. If you can do both, that's a great start.*

*Classic mistakes by ambitious new-in-role law firm CMO's are:*

- *Seeking recognition and relationships among the partners to exclude their marketing and BD team; even worse, taking credit for their success.*

- *Not getting in the trenches with the team by occupying a strategic 'ivory tower' and avoiding any participation in operations!*

- *You are equating strong leadership with command and control.*

*The average Senior Partner of a law firm wants five things from their CMO:*

- *A strong brand and a good reputation*

- *A clear and articulated service portfolio*

- *New clients*

- *Strong relationships with existing clients*

- *A high-performing, loyal marketing and BD function*

*Some partners will believe they know more about marketing and BD than you do. But don't let that stop you evangelising the value of marketing to them every day - tell the success stories, and open their eyes to what good marketing and BD looks like.*

*Get your team aligned with the firm's strategy. Take some time to understand, with them, what it will take from the marketing and BD team to deliver the firm's strategic priorities. Then take a rain check occasionally to test whether the time and money invested in daily projects and activities contribute to delivering those priorities.*

*As CMO, treat your team as professional experts in marketing and BD. Hold them up as experts among the partners. Encourage partners to develop individual or team BD plans with senior marketing and BD team members. Then make sure that partners are recognised for delivering on those plans in their reviews. That's a strong foundation for a successful collaboration between lawyers, marketing, and BD people."*

## Transitioning into a Chief Operating Officer (COO) role

An outstanding CMO has the opportunity in their firm to transition their role into a COO position; as a successful CMO, you already must understand all aspects of client relationships, firm strategy and pricing.

The key to becoming a successful CMO is to gain management buy-in and peer engagement across your firm [see **CHAPTER 10**]. The CMO role now focuses beyond just marketing into the client experience - which is infinitely broader. The whole firm needs to embrace customer experience to make that experience truly exceptional. Marketers can't deliver customer experience alone. Other departments - IT, Finance and Technology, play a critical role in delivering outcomes. Therefore, CMOs must collaborate with other senior executives to provide customer experience results.

They are looking beyond the Marketing function and being intellectually curious about how all the pieces of a business fit together is essential to operating in a leadership position within a professional services firm [see **CHAPTER 9**].

---

## Expert view

Astrid Altmann Forbes, Chief Operating Officer - Germany at Linklaters, based in Munich:

---

*"As a COO building business strategy and integration, functional work to support the strategy requires connecting lots of dots and breaking down silos. During my 20+ years in the industry, several key elements have served me well in arriving at this point: my curiosity and appetite for learning, being prepared to step out of my comfort zone and; a strong network.*

*Having spent most of my career to date in strategy, business development and marketing, I have always taken a great interest in understanding how a professional service firm's business model works, following market trends, in particular how clients' demands evolve and what part Marketing takes in delivering the firm's strategic plan. I encourage my teams to really understand the firm's /strategy for each of its services, constantly challenge any new idea, whether it adds value to advancing the firm or practice, to take an interest in how other functions are playing their part and how by collaborating with other business teams we can provide an even better service.*

*This holistic view of the firm's business has proved invaluable for me moving into a general management role and leading a team of subject matter experts in areas that I have not worked in previously.*

*Further, I always actively pursued opportunities to push my boundaries, very often beyond my comfort zone. The unfamiliarity of a new set of responsibilities can be daunting at first. Demonstrating a genuine interest, being humble, asking a myriad of questions and actively listening, in the beginning, will make you succeed and help you grow as a person and, of course, will equip you with new skills and knowledge, which in turn will help you advance your career."*

 **Key points to remember**

1. CMOs are still relatively new positions within the industry, and firms are increasingly adding marketing representation to their boards, a testament to the rising importance of the position.

2. The role has developed dramatically and is increasing in importance as firms adapt to globalisation, define their markets, and implement go-to-market strategies to remain competitive.

3. The pressure to demonstrate results and return on investment is immense as a CMO. It has always been difficult for marketing to measure the impact of their activities, but this is now more important than ever.

4. The CMO role now focuses beyond just marketing into the client experience - which is infinitely broader. Therefore, CMOs must collaborate with other senior executives, e.g. IT, to provide customer experience results.

# 5

# The CMO of Tomorrow

*"I do not believe you can do today's job with yesterday's methods
and be in business tomorrow"*
*—Horatio Nelson Jackson*

With Marketing's role evolving, CMOs carry a more significant amount of responsibility and influence over a firm's strategy. It is crucial to plan your career carefully. If you wish to be a CMO, you must step outside your comfort zone, expose yourself to situations, and challenges that will help prepare you for such a role.

To understand what is expected of you in this role and what skills will be needed to be a successful CMO today and in the future. I interviewed several first-time CMOs and seasoned CMOs in professional services firms about their career and what skills you should develop now to serve them in the future as a CMO. Additionally, I received input from two senior partners, who shared their perspectives on what future senior management teams will expect from CMOs.

**Expert view**    Nora Shearer, CMO at Shearman & Sterling, based in New York:

*"The role of the CMO has dramatically evolved over the years, and expectations surrounding the position continue to grow. A successful CMO today needs to have a great understanding of a firm's strategy, practices,*

*lawyers, and a deep understanding of the business of law. The CMO of today is someone who can wear both the "creative" and the "business" hat. Someone who can execute the brand's look and feel and understand revenue growth models, digitalisation, and data analytics.*

*During my legal marketing career, I was fortunate to combine my business development and marketing background and utilise my financial knowledge to deliver a strategy that maximises impact and provides growth. I expect that as technology continues to evolve and challenge the way we work, greater collaboration will exist among business services. Most important for the CMO of the future is to be open to new ideas and adaptable in an ever-changing environment that requires a constant appetite and energy for learning."*

## Demonstrating ROI and establishing a metrics culture

An incredible amount of stress on verifying outcomes and ROI, in the role. Marketers have always struggled to measure the results of their efforts in the industry, and it is now more critical than ever for you to do so. Firms today control all costs intelligently, marketing budgets are getting tighter, and the CFO is always looking at marketing expenses. To be a genuinely strategic CMO, therefore, one must transform the mindset of the entire firm and partnership.

With digital marketing, you have access to powerful new tools and metrics to gauge the success of your marketing initiatives. In your role, the more you can demonstrate a direct connection between spending and revenues, the more success you will have in the boardroom. However, there are still elements of the position, such as measuring the precise contribution of digital marketing and social media to fee generation and the bottom line, which creates immediate pressure on you to cut what is not, to focus on more immediate ROI initiatives.

In professional service firms, executive committees criticise marketers for not understanding the implications of their actions. I spoke with a CMO who expressed frustration that while every other function in the company is reinventing itself, Marketing is still perceived to rely too heavily on research and creative execution rather than catalysts for new developments and direction.

Due to the legacy of the "silo" structure in firms and Marketing's perception as an expense centre, you will need to demonstrate, as a CMO, that marketing can be a driving force for growth and profitability.

Gain the support and respect of your board by demonstrating data-driven evidence of success. Rather than focusing on more complex concepts that those outside marketing do not understand, such as your firm's share of the market and brand equity, instead turning your focus to your firm's P&L or financial ROI.

## Expert view

Heather Reid, Chief Business Development and Marketing Officer at Miles & Stockbridge P.C., based in Baltimore:

*"A strong CMO in 2022 (and beyond) will be working hand in hand with the CFO, CHRO, COO, and CTO and is an integral part of the team that drives the organisation's success at every level. Firm leadership is looking for the CMO to fit in well with the rest of the Chiefs. Your skillset needs to go beyond marketing and business development, to have a firm grasp on how the firm operates, navigate key political relationships and offer key critical insights and suggestions for overall operational success – and be able to measure that success with precise data analytics and KPIs.*

*Not "new", however, COVID-19 continues to force CMO's to reimagine how we respond to both and catapult their importance to the top of the list.*

*My advice to those stepping into this new role is to remember this mantra, 'Small Consistent Daily Actions'.*

*Everyone thinks that to be a wildly successful CMO is a result of some big "aha" moment or radical new idea. Some revelation that "Yes, this is it - I've figured it all out!" We tend to view these as "lucky" executives who made a life-changing decision one random day, and boom - their career (and firm) is suddenly on a new and successful path. The thing is that is rarely the case and also a dangerous mindset for your mental health. Focus on incremental daily progress (negative or positive) because that causes transformation. Showing up, every single day, doing what you say you are going to do, listening for feedback on how to do it differently tomorrow, building the personal connections, laying the groundwork - this understated, and frequently unglamorous work, is how you make an impact and transform your team. Focus on the small changes - they add up to big success."*

## Tech collaboration is key to growth

IT builds and controls the technology that powers and runs the Marketing department in professional service firms, e.g. the website, hubs, apps, and other digital infrastructure that enables client data gathering, analytics, and BD purposes. As a result, the adoption of marketing technology and digital processes can become bogged down in battles over ownership, budget, and credit.

A new normal has now emerged, with significant implications for how buyers and sellers do business in the future - highlighted digital transformation as one of their leading priorities for the next 12 months.

In my conversations with several CMOs, I heard that what started as a crisis response to COVID-19 *"forced B2B buyers and sellers to go digital in a big way."* The Marketing team needs to know big data and AI models the same way they create beautiful campaigns, digital platforms, and services. Each agreed that *"analytics are playing an increasingly critical role."*

Keeping up with trends, technologies, and methodologies working for similar companies by speaking with other marketing leaders was something each of them said they are increasingly doing.

**Expert view**    Adriana Giometti, Chief Marketing and Client Relations Officer at Holman Webb. CMO of the Year 2018 & 2020 Finalist - CEO Magazine Awards, based in Sydney:

*"To be a future CMO in the industry you have to be a social and customer behaviour expert, but need to think like a Chief Technology Officer (CTO) also. The role of the CMO will be less obscure and a lot more quantifiable as we engage more data and metrics around the Customer Experience Metrics (CX) and BD process, going forward.*

*Driving the strategic vision of your firm and leading the focus on overall customer engagement is crucial to cultivating your brand as a CMO. In this role you need to be data-driven, highly strategic and visionary futurists.*

*The future CMO role is unique because you will need to know the client like no other C-suite executive in the team. It requires fast shifts in the firm's strategy, and you will be responsible for delivering that message to the Partners. You will need to be confident, intuitive and highly credible. Ultimately, these elements cultivate your brand. It needs to reflect that you are a thought leader and expert in your field. Ideally, you will be on speaking circuits, publish articles, have valuable networks and have excellent mentoring and leadership skills. Every aspect of personal branding expected of partners within a firm will also apply to the CMO!"*

## Building relationships

The relationship-building strategies of B2C and B2B companies differ. The products offered by B2B companies require specialised knowledge and fostering relationships with clients to generate revenue for firms. As we move into the digital age, Marketing functions focus more on lead generation and business development. It is increasingly common for

CMOs to act as "chief growth officers" without having the authority or resources that come with the title.

As your firm's CMO increasingly your role is expanding outside of traditional marketing and focusing more on driving growth for your firm. CMOs I talked to who are members of their executive committee all agreed that their task for 2022 is to pursue disruptive growth. The CMO position is often considered the executive responsible for driving disruptive change.

## Expert view

Tamara Box, Managing Partner (Europe & Middle East) and sits on the global board at Reed Smith, based in London:

*"Good marketing starts with two activities: insight and listening. CMOs and those wanting to take on this role should excel in these two areas, in my view:*

- *We get an in-depth understanding of our clients' businesses through market research – what products/services they offer, who their customers are, and their competitive advantages. Critically, while these are also the same things that a CMO should know about our own business, our business is not our marketing focus. We have to view the world through the client's eyes to see how we contribute to their success. Therefore, the CMO must understand this and become the firm's client champion.*

- *And that's where the listening comes in. Good CMOs ensure that we talk to our clients to find out their priorities, where their challenges lie, and what they see happening to their marketplace in the future. How can we help them?*

*In reality, the client probably doesn't need to hear about us—how old our firm is, how many professionals we have in each area, our office locations, or anything else that sounds like self-promotion. The client only wants to hear about the client. What will that mean if that client works with our firm for their business? What will their business look like in 2022 or five years hence? How will their profitability improve or their market position rise? A great CMO will ensure that this is the orientation of the professionals within our firm.*

*Remember, marketing isn't about what you want to sell but what the client wants to buy. The best CMOs know to make sure we always remember this."*

## Marketing continues to be decentralised

Marketing spending and decisions are highly decentralised at a large firm with multiple service areas, multiple geographic focuses and sectors. In such environments according to Strategy&, the CMO may control on average only around 15 to 20 percent of the company's total marketing budget. The other 80 to 85 per cent rests in the hands of the individual lines of business.

Often global professional service firms, for example, each territory and practice funds and manages its marketing budget. The result is duplication of effort, inconsistency, and incoherence in marketing strategy.

The discrepancies and duplication can further fracture the relationship between marketing and its internal stakeholder base. When stakeholders cannot get what they want from marketing or have disparate needs across the firm, they carve out budgets to hire and maintain their Marketing teams, budgets and objectives.

## Immersed in tactical issues and distant from strategy.

Marketing is often restricted to providing client collateral and managing creative execution rather than being involved in more strategic areas such as the client journey or developing new products. A report published in

2019 stated that in many B2B organisations, tactical activities are where 70 per cent of the time marketing is spent and only 30 per cent on strategic activities.

Patterns like this have a cascading effect. The professional services marketing industry has always been short of seasoned marketing professionals with deep knowledge of complex products, the competitive landscape, and strategic skills. However, by relegating marketing to tactical and generalist roles, those individuals won't develop strategic insight and direction to help the company grow. In these firms, junior marketing professionals are often jacks-of-all-trades rather than developing valuable specialised skills - all the more difficult due to the ongoing problem of attracting and retaining talent.

Suppose you're a CMO on your firm's board. In that case, you should not limit your opinions on strategy solely to marketing-related matters. You are increasingly expected in your role as the firm's CMO to add value across broader issues the board needs to address.

## Expert view

Tim Corcoran, a former CEO, now guides law firm and law department leaders through the profitable disruption of outdated business models. Principal at Corcoran Consulting Group, based in Virginia:

*"An accomplished recruiter who had placed many law firm CMOs once tried to convince me that a law degree is the most important credential for a CMO, or a track record of unflinching service to the needs of partners will suffice. A veteran CMO of several leading law firms advised younger colleagues to never say no to a partner and wait at least a year before making a suggestion. They were right. That is, if the CMO's goal is to blindly serve partner whims without regard to business impact because law firms are inevitably successful, they were right.*

*But as the market has painfully learned, modern law firms are complex businesses operating in competitive markets, serving demanding clients with numerous options to address their needs. The legal market needs professional marketers.*

*A modern law firm CMO has experience and training in business, management, and leadership. Because they create better alternatives, embrace long-range planning, and thrive in short-term chaos, they're willing to say no, and they like to challenge others.*

*It's a thrilling ride, and it's not for everyone. Thankfully."*

## Capture the essence of the firm's culture and capabilities

Developing a strategy that provides a sustainable advantage for your firm is a challenge. As your firm's CMO you play a leading role in advising the board and the wider organisation on clarifying and defining its firm brand and culture in a way that creates a differentiation strategy geared for growth.

You must become client-centric rather than firm-centric to do this effectively. It requires you to gather feedback from your clients to understand what they are saying and what is resonating with them already and then determine what your firm can offer in value that no competitor can. Once you have done this, you must communicate this internally to get the entire firm into the vision and articulate these capabilities to your clients.

**Expert view**    Chris Saul, Managing Director at advisory firm Christopher Saul Associates and former senior partner at Slaughter and May, based in London:

*"I believe the role of the CMO in a professional services firm is to capture the essence of the firm's culture and capabilities and present those elements to the outside world in a compelling manner. I can break it down into several parts:*

- *How, in a few short sentences, can the distinctive nature of the firm be captured? Without resorting unduly to generic terms such as "high quality" and "solutions orientated", how best to convey the real personality of the firm?*

- *What are the new and evolving client and practice opportunities? A current example would be ESG. Is the firm's ESG proposition well-articulated, and what are the Top 10 client opportunities in this space?*

- *Do the firm's relationships with its clients get refreshed regularly? Are its publications – and its website – interesting, modern and engaging? Are its events appealing?*

- *Are the partners effectively reaching the optimal range of influencers – the legal directories, legal and business journalists, and fellow intermediaries such as investment bankers and peer law firms in other jurisdictions?*

- *Are the firm's pitch documents well-honed and differentiated? What can the Marketing team do to help the partners develop their presentation skills?*

*The CMO and the wider Marketing team are instrumental in helping the partners to articulate, focus and convey, to best effect, the firm's essential proposition."*

## The Future of the CMO for professional service firms

You need the ability to adapt at lightning speed, disrupt the industry, and own lead generation and brand building in an increasingly fragmented industry. In this fluid world of constant uncertainty, if you embrace change, understand your brand significance, and create value for your firm, you will be looked to for marketing transformation by the board.

The CMO of tomorrow understands that great client experiences translate directly to bottom-line results. CMOs need to focus on building competent teams that can deliver ROI and create KPIs for internal stakeholders that put the client at the very centre of your firm's thinking.

Whether you are at the start of your career, stepping into your first management position, or a seasoned CMO, you must develop the skills necessary to make the transition possible and understand the pressures and challenges that come with the top job.

---

**Expert view**   Luke Ferrandino, Chief Marketing Officer at Paul, Weiss, Rifkind, Wharton & Garrison LLP, based in New York:

---

*"When I started my career in legal marketing more than 20 years ago, I worked in a department of five people at Davis Polk. Back then, two people (I was one of them) covered practice area support, and we mainly focused on matter promotion, pitches and directory submissions. We had one communication person and one writer. And the head of the department was a "jack of all trades" who led special projects across the firm.*

*At present, I lead a team of approximately 60 people specialising in various areas, from sales and lead generation to client development and retention, media relations, internal communications, business analytics, technology, digital marketing, alumni relations, events, and business intelligence. We are not unique, and the legal industry's marketing and business development departments have grown as we have demonstrated the value we can bring to our firms and our clients.*

*To predict where the legal marketing industry will be in the next 20 years is impossible. Still, I may know a few truths about what it will take to be a successful CMO for the future in the professional services industry:*

- *Get an advanced business degree – whether an MBA or specialised training in finance, marketing, communications, statistics and data analysis, technical industry, or other areas of relevance, you need to be the expert of your area of focus. Just as our clients expect lawyers to be specialists in their fields, so must we be in ours.*

- *Learn to love maths – firms are much more data-oriented than they used to be. At Paul, Weiss, we use specific metrics to measure our marketing strategies. With the advancement of technology and tools available to law firms, this position will continue to be critical in the years to come. Also, it is crucial to understand law firm finance – you have to know how your firms make money to contribute to the bottom line.*

- *Speak the lawyer's language – while you don't need to be an expert in every practice capability, you need to have a foundational understanding of your firm's work, who does that work, and why they get hired for the work they do. Read as much as you can about your firm and find projects that can help expose you at a deeper level to these practices.*

- *Speak to, and listen to your clients – more and more CMOs and their team members are client-facing, and many firms invest in sales teams. Learn how to speak to clients and put their feedback into action to enhance the relationship.*

- *Don't be afraid to experiment – be bold and find the right opportunities to experiment with new ideas or approaches, whether testing a new process to create potential efficiencies or kicking the tires on a unique approach to generating leads. The only way we continue to evolve is by stretching ourselves.*

- *Lead by example – the buck stops with the CMO. You have a responsibility to the firm, its lawyers, and you are also responsible for the success of every single member of your team. Support the people who report to you at all costs, position them to be successful, and protect them so that they can safely experiment to flourish and grow.*

*Above all else, be curious – while we may know to a degree where our industry may head in the future, we can't possibly know everything. Be prepared and seek different opinions and perspectives on everything from market trends to micro strategies and tactics. Read newspapers and trade journals. And if you nurture a robust relationship network in your early years in the industry, it will pay dividends later by having a reservoir of knowledge to tap into when you need it most."*

**Key points to remember**

1. As a CMO, your role has evolved in the Industry, meaning you now have a much broader amount of responsibility and influence over a firm's strategy.

2. It is becoming increasingly critical for you to expand your role beyond traditional marketing and drive growth in your organisation. CMOs are increasingly acting as "chief growth officers" without the authority or resources associated with that title.

3. The Marketing team must understand big data and AI models in the same way they create beautiful campaigns and digital platforms.

4. Your board will support and respect you if you show them data-driven evidence of your success. It's more effective to focus on your firm's P&L or financial ROI instead of more complex concepts that outside marketing doesn't understand. For example, your firm's share of the market or brand equity.

# PART TWO

## Alignment with your firm's strategy

*"If you want to improve the organisation, you have to improve yourself, and the organisation gets pulled up with you"*
*—Indra Nooyi*

Firms and their Marketing functions have never been more essential than they are right now. The professional services industry continues to focus on creating client value to sustain long-term growth, whilst the market continues to be aggressively competitive, requiring you to identify the correct areas to focus on to position your firm to be relevant to your clients.

To position your firm for maximum growth now and in the future, you will need to approach your work and career strategically. The key to this is focusing on the bigger strategic picture rather than focusing too much on the tactics.

Perhaps this has come up in a recent performance review or is a crucial requirement listed for a senior-level job description you have seen recently. The importance of becoming more skilled at strategic thinking is something that your firm and line manager will be demanding of you to move up into senior positions. When your manager is asking you to be "more strategic", they want you to build on the great tactical work you are doing already and further demonstrate how what you are doing contributes to the bigger picture (aligned to your firm's objectives) and how you are specifically adding real value to the firm.

The key to this is knowing the bigger picture in the first place. This requires you to understand how your firm is performing in the industry, identify external trends and consider how these impact your firm. It is vital that you possess such knowledge and consistently apply this.

Firms traditionally refer to the Marketing function as "support." Considered by stakeholders as "doers" and "order-takers" rather than ones that lead the organisation. As a result, it is challenging for marketers to be considered strategic in their roles. Rather than being sought out for big picture thinking, we focus more on the tactical elements of our roles.

At each of the firms I have worked at during my career, I have learned the following values set out in this section of the book that continues to guide me today, and I strive to embody them in my role as a senior manager. From an assistant level to my current position, I can look back on a number of them as crucial factors in my career advancement and ongoing performance.

You are likely doing many of these without realising it. Embracing these values and incorporating them into your current role will give you greater control over the tasks you undertake, your approach to them, and how you add value to your internal stakeholders.

You must look beyond the specifics of any initiative you are tasked with within your role and take time to learn how that particular project aligns with the firm's growth strategy. By developing an understanding in this area, you will be able to utilise your tactical skill set with a more significant strategic awareness that your line manager and senior stakeholders across the business will no doubt notice, and you will be considered for advancement and greater responsibility in the future, as they will want to depend on you.

# 6

# Critical thinking and knowledge

*"It's a dirty little secret. Most executives cannot articulate the objective, scope, and advantage of their business in a simple statement. If they can't, neither can anyone else"*
—David J. Collis and Michael G. Rukstad

## Big Picture Thinking

It is essential to understand your firm's strategy to manage your time effectively. There are times when you feel as though your inbox and workload are endless, and with each new request, your priorities shift. You will struggle to make the right impact in your firm if you cannot step back and take a holistic look at what you are doing and what you need to be doing.

At professional services firms, you might find yourself overworked, managing a flurry of requests imposed by individual stakeholders. To become more strategic, one must *pursue the vital few over the trivial many*.

Changing marketing initiatives without evaluating whether you will reach your firm's objectives will not enhance your clout with senior stakeholders focused on these objectives. You will be better able to focus on the most impactful tasks if you describe why you are doing something and the ROI anticipated and achieved.

Therefore, you must periodically review your firm's strategy and sit down with your line manager to check how your objectives and tasks align with this. Concentrate your energy and focus on tasks that will help you increase your career prospects and get noticed internally.

The same behaviour that we heard from CMOs worldwide when creating this book was to gain a solid understanding of what your firm does and who your clients are. Suppose you do not keep yourself curious and challenge yourself to learn more about your firm's offers. In that case, you will limit the output and success of your marketing efforts and define your career advancement within the industry.

---

### In practice

A common mistake I regularly see with those wanting to become a manager is that often individuals become too linear in their focus.

You must continue to learn what other areas of the firm are thriving or dovetailing. It can be straightforward for you to focus just on your role; "that is not my role, so I don't know anything that can help you". To be someone your stakeholders turn to for advice and guidance, you must find solutions for their problems. To do this, you need to make sure you invest your time learning about other services and areas at your firm.

---

## How well do you know your company?

The Cambridge Business English Dictionary defines commercial awareness as *"the knowledge of how businesses make money, what customers want, and what problems there are in a particular area of business."* Therefore, to be successful, you need to know your firm's strengths and weaknesses to apply that information to make sensible decisions.

Can you answer the following questions directly if one of your key stakeholders asked you? Are you clear about these points?

- What is your business knowledge, the services you offer clients, competitors and brand positions?
- Your vision, mission, culture, and business plan?
- Strategy towards diversity & inclusion, environment, philanthropic?
- Do you take the time to read important news about your firm at least once a week, if not daily?

Mark Murphy, CEO of LeadershipIQ, states that *"to obtain power in your organisation, you have to have the answers to other people's questions"*. To do this, you need to understand where your firm is going; once you know this, you can advise others and help form the strategy to help your firm get there. It is worth reviewing the answers to the above questions for future conversations with external and internal stakeholders.

---

## Expert view

Deborah Brightman Farone, a former CMO at Cravath, Swaine & Moore, and a marketing strategy consultant (Farone Advisors LLC) based in New York:

---

*"In doing my research, the one complaint I hear about mid-level marketers is that they don't know the intricacies of the practice or sector that they are responsible for marketing, as well as they should. While the basis of the remark may be genuine or it may be a matter of the lawyers' perception, there is a tendency with most marketers to rush into developing the tactics of marketing, including press interviews, seminars and content development.*

*We all share that drive to show results. I would recommend you use at least an hour of your time each week to learn more about the area you aim to market. That may mean going to an industry or sector group meeting, speaking with a partner about how they won their last several clients or asking if you can sit in on a new business conversation with a client. It is essential to continue the self-education process, and to demonstrate your interest, even when you have a full plate."*

---

## (There's) no such thing as a stupid question

Often, it is difficult to admit when you don't understand something or aren't sure what to do next. When working with knowledgeable individuals, you might feel very embarrassed, especially when discussing overly technical topics. However, the worst thing you can do is pretend to understand something and not ask for further clarification where needed.

For example after a group meeting, arrange a follow-up discussion with those who did not understand the shared information and ensure you have captured crucial points and actions from the call.

Since email is quick and convenient, it can be easy to hide behind it for most communication in junior positions where busy stakeholder teams across the company are sending you requests. Although this approach is practical, exchanging emails back and forth can waste time and annoy stakeholders. Consider picking up the phone or scheduling a meeting to discuss; this way, you can ask many questions to clarify exactly what is needed and how you will be held accountable.

When you next encounter something you are unsure about, don't be afraid to ask questions to gain a deeper understanding. If you don't know the answer, no question is stupid. You will save a lot of wasted time, which is a more embarrassing and damaging outcome than admitting you don't know something.

In overly technical topics, is it best to seek clarification to ensure that you fully comprehend and understand why the information is pertinent to your client base? Below you will find a valuable framework for understanding technical topics.

## Understanding technical topics

Unless you have made a career switch from an advisor role, it is doubtful that you are educated and therefore understand in-depth certain technical areas essential to directing marketing efforts. To market better to clients, these are strategies for better understanding technical topics:

- **Why should the client care?** - to understand a topic, you must first identify the target audience and consider why they find it interesting. Identifying which clients would find a topic relevant is critical to selecting the suitable marketing channels to communicate this topic to them.
- **Focus on the business impact, not detail** - you don't need to fully understand the technical information about a particular topic, just how or why it will affect your target audience's business, helping you to gain their attention by emphasising these points in your marketing communications.
- **Speak the language-specific** technical topics have lots of jargon, metaphors and acronyms, so you must try to understand specific terms and find out what certain acronyms mean. Using these in your communication will help you engage with internal and external stakeholders.

## Thinking outside of the box

It is easy to constantly monitor and respond to what your competitors are doing in your industry due to its competitive nature. Do your partners often share marketing that your competitors produce and ask you to replicate it?

Directories, awards, or other industry rankings do not help such behaviour, further intensifying competitiveness. Partners are encouraged to compete and pay close attention to what their peers are doing. Although what is shared and what competitors are doing may be interesting, it is often not too different from your firm's current activities.

To differentiate your firm's brand and gain a competitive advantage, you should broaden your perspective outside of the industry, e.g. legal, accounting, property or any other service, instead of taking inspiration and ideas from other B2B brands outside of the industry.

Pay close attention to how they communicate their brand, the channels they use, and how they deliver a client-centric experience. To act as their client and experience their marketing the same way their clients do, follow their LinkedIn page and subscribe to their mailing lists to keep you updated with their latest campaigns and marketing communications.

Another source of ideas is from your network. I am fortunate to have many classmates from university who hold various marketing roles across different industries, so I am often able to pick their brains and understand innovative approaches they are implementing to gain a competitive advantage. If you don't have many contacts in the industry, you can focus on developing such a network to help you in the future [see **CHAPTER 20**].

To further develop your commercial awareness, you should be engaging with business news daily and resources in your industry, regularly reviewing global publications like the FT, Bloomberg, and other online sites, business blogs and news broadcasts. As you keep up with various industry developments, think about how each change will affect your firm and the clients you serve, focusing primarily on how it could affect the type of work you'll be doing in your position of choice at the firm.

---

## Expert view

Tis Dias, Director - Global Head of Client & Market Development (Corporates) at Clifford Chance, based in London:

---

*"Don't you find that some of the best people you have ever worked with in professional services marketing are also the ones that constantly bring into the firm what they learn from outside the firm, and do so in a way that, more often than not, prompts you and your Partners to take a long, hard look in the mirror?*

*These people often think about past experiences and how these experiences relate to their current environment. They make time to learn about different businesses, markets, industries, and technologies. They pick their moments wisely to share their insights. They communicate with impact and high energy. They demonstrate a passion for learning and sharing knowledge that rubs off positively on all those around them.*

*These are the people who often stop me in my tracks and prompt me to think about what I'm doing - such an invaluable and precious commodity in my view.*

*I would encourage you to look over the parapet (beyond their day-to-day roles) at other organisations and industries and develop your knowledge outside of your practice area or business line; the more outstanding your overall contribution will be to your firm."*

## Client Discovery

Do you often create fantastic marketing but have not considered whether your clients need it? The importance of empathy in your role is one of the most important behaviours to become strategic. If you are not in a client-facing position or have exposure to clients, it can be challenging to put yourself in the shoes of a client to understand your target audience's priorities. Frustratingly, professional services are an industry where the end client's often removed from the Marketing function.

It is rare to interact directly with clients. The internal partners who interact directly with clients may not always feed this insight back to marketing, which leaves you mostly guessing or following stakeholder suggestions blindly, hoping this leads to positive engagement and results.

Although a 100+ page thought leadership report that has taken months to produce might look aesthetically pleasing and the technical coverage of the topic may satisfy your internal stakeholders, does the client have time to read it? Are they able to apply that knowledge to their role to make life easier?

Instead of making grand predictions, it is crucial that you consistently seek to understand your client's needs better. If your firm doesn't readily allow you access to talk to clients, there are a few clever ways to understand the client perspective still:

- **Alumni** - when your former partners and associates move in-house, make sure you remain in contact.

- **Client-facing individuals** - identify several partners who meet with clients regularly (rainmakers) and pick their brains regularly.

- **On loan idea generators** - occasionally, advisors are sent to clients on secondment, particularly in the legal industry. Try to build and develop relationships with these individuals when they return, but most importantly, whilst they are there. They are a fantastic source of insight as they understand your firm and what the client is tackling internally.

- **Resources** - consider what your clients read and contribute to, and ensure that you read, listen and engage with these resources to understand them better.

- **Create client-facing opportunities** - you might be running a conference or a significant event where you meet clients at networking sessions or build relationships over email when responding to clients. These examples create interactions with clients and ways to keep in touch. Currently, with the shift to virtual marketing, you can attend specific client seminars or training and hear their opinions. When you are skilled in digital and audio/visual, partners often seek you to ensure virtual client-facing events will run smoothly, which means you will be involved in these.

- **Connect with clients** - marketers still find it difficult to connect with clients they've interacted with previously. LinkedIn is an excellent tool for connecting with contacts you have engaged with through marketing initiatives or client-facing engagement. I recommend using LinkedIn to connect with contacts and clients regularly. Also reaching out to people I am interested in learning more about or connecting with, even if we have never met before. Avoid using the default connection request message; instead, create a personalised message tailored towards the individual you want to connect with.

When it comes to the tasks you are involved with, it's essential to be open-minded and put the client first in planning and executing these tasks. You should always ask yourself and others, *"how does this help our clients, and why should they care about this?"*. If you can answer these questions, you can be confident that what you're planning and delivering is in the clients' best interests.

## In practice

When I joined Eversheds Sutherland in a client-facing role for the Industrials sector, I did so with limited previous exposure to clients other than the infrequent interaction at client events and other client pleasantries through email I had experienced in previous firms. Yet, I was required to know what our clients needed and respond to these. With little to no contacts that worked in-house, this task was all the more difficult.

To change this and develop a deep understanding of our clients' industry requirements, I began cultivating a network of contacts in the sector. I specifically focused on leveraging LinkedIn to follow our clients and got in the habit of connecting with our clients on LinkedIn. Initially reluctant to do this, I was surprised at how receptive contacts were in connecting with me as I had not met many of them.

Through doing this, I monitored and interacted with our clients, which developed my understanding of the clients operating in the sector, which ultimately shaped our sector's marketing strategy. Going one step further, I began reaching out to clients with ideas and getting their input into ongoing initiatives, which allowed me to focus on what we were doing and ensure that our output as a sector Marketing team was relevant to our target audience. This approach is evidence that I had previously created initiatives for clients, in my earlier career roles in a vacuum from the client and reliant upon others telling me what clients needed.

Check out your connections when you have an exciting idea or want some feedback. If you are responsible for certain jurisdictions, services or sectors, identify someone who matches your target audience. The template below will allow you to connect with clients on LinkedIn.

## How to write an effective LinkedIn connection request

*Hello [insert their first name],*

*I wanted to connect with you because I saw that you worked at Y, a company I am interested in following and keeping informed about since [insert your firm] frequently works in your sector.*

*I am working on an idea that I think would interest companies like [insert their company]. Before launching the project, I would like to get your thoughts to ensure it is relevant to you and similar clients.*

*Best*

*[insert your name]*

## Expert view
Ian Cohn, Head of Clients at Eversheds Sutherland, based in London:

*"What is it that clients most want law firms to improve in their client relationships? Recent research by Thomson Reuters, BTI Consulting, Wicker*

*Park and others all deliver the same message – 'Understand our business, understand our industry'. It's the most significant impact on client relationships when professional service firms get it right. That's not just about the lead partner getting it right – it's about the whole client service team showing they understand the client. Good business development professionals can make such an impact; by becoming the firm's expert on the client's business and industry and applying that knowledge across the client relationship.*

*An excellent way to better understand your firm's key clients is to consider and think of their organisation from an investor's perspective.*

*For each client, ask yourself, "Why buy shares in this company?". It is frequently a critical question that a Chief Executive Officer has to answer every day to their shareholders. By trying to answer this question, you are finding out what makes the company valuable, what risks the board needs to manage, and how they try to differentiate their products and services in the market.*

*Review a client's annual report, equity research notes prepared by investment banks, and other available information prepared for their shareholders. All this will tell you about a client's strategy, geographical focus, market priorities and main business risks. In other words, it's an excellent blueprint for developing a client plan that responds directly to the company's strategic focus.*

*Look at the work your firm is currently doing for that organisation; how much of that work can you link to their business strategy and critical risks? Look at the gaps between your job and the client's overall business activities. What business activities is your firm not involved in? Which of those best fit your firm's expertise in that client's industry? Put those two data points together, and there is your growth plan!*

*Identify other clients in the same industry, and look at the firm's work for those clients. What type of work is growing, and what is driving the demand for that work? That will help you understand the dynamics of the industry sector and is excellent knowledge to take back to your client service team.*

*Finally, take any opportunity to speak to clients directly and check your understanding of their strategy. That could be members of their legal team or business people you encounter at industry events. Ask them about their area of the business. Good questions include 'Where are you currently seeing growth in the business?', 'What risks have your team identified around executing the strategy?', and 'What additional pressures are the legal team experiencing from the current market environment?'.*

*The professional services market is competitive, with every firm ultimately working to serve its clients. If you do not have a complete picture of your client's needs and business, you will struggle to market to them and develop opportunities for your firm.*

*The above approach will help you to understand your clients better and how your firm's services can help them achieve their objectives."*

## Take a step back and prioritise

*"If you don't have time, the truth is, you don't have priorities"*

—TIM FERRISS

Sometimes your inbox can seem to be overflowing with work, requiring you to concentrate on categorising these requests to determine which are urgent, important, the information you need to read at some point and those that you can actually ignore, and or delegate to others.

It is not until you move into senior roles that you quickly realise that busy and productive are not the same. Often, junior professionals in the sector try to do many things and accomplish them in short turnarounds, which can be exhausting and not sustainable. Being means ruthlessly prioritising and carrying out the essential tasks effectively.

In your role, you will be required to react quickly to fast-changing events, which is a crucial skill you need to develop. Doing this well, and what will set you apart from others, will be taking a step back and using this time to think and react in the best way to produce quality output, rather than reactive and fast work.

It is counterproductive and costly to have an unchecked sense of urgency. By reacting too quickly, you could end up making short-sighted decisions or adopting the wrong solutions, ignoring underlying causes and causing collateral damage.

Another unconscious tendency to be aware of and focus less on is those tasks that you enjoy or know you are good at, particularly at the expense of your highest priorities.

Reacting quickly to fast-changing events is undoubtedly a valuable skill. However, what increasingly sets the best apart is the ability to be responsive whilst also finding time to think; to produce quality work, not just fast work.

## In practice

I regularly experience moments now and in previous roles when the to-do list seems endless, and your inbox continues to overflow with new requests that pull you away from what matters and will advance your career. In moments like this, I almost feel paralysed and can spend wasted time stressing over what to do next and can end up doing nothing.

One approach I had always found the key to combating this destructive behaviour and taking back control is something my father taught me when I shadowed him as part of my work experience whilst I was at school. My father was a Finance Director and was accountable for several important tasks at any one time that would be key to the company's long-term growth objectives. I often saw him take a blank piece of paper and write a handful of the tasks on his to-do list that he knew were urgent or crucial to his objectives. He would then score them from an A–C, with an A being critical and had to be done today before anything else; a B would be essential but possibly not urgent so could be got to when he had done the A's on the list. Anything categorised as a C could almost be put back on the to-do list for another day.

A simple approach, but this is what makes this all the more effective when you are overwhelmed by your workload, and by not taking control, you will become stressed and fall behind.

You can use other similar urgent-important metrics, such as The Eisenhower Matrix, which I have seen many partners use to manage their workload.

## Strategic planning

Even though your objectives are clearly defined, it's sometimes challenging to ensure that your time focuses on those tasks that will help you accomplish them. Avoid being reactive all the time.

By stepping back, you'll be able to manage your workload better and ensure you don't become overwhelmed by the wrong types of tasks, which will impede your advancement in your role. The challenges you will face at work are many and varied. Still, it is essential to ensure that you focus on the right initiatives you are measured and rewarded on that ultimately enhance your promotion prospects.

Take a step back and commit to regular thinking time and doing it in the following ways:

- **Following up on meetings** - after every meeting, you can collect a lot of notes and items for your to-do list. Revisit these notes later in the day and focus on adding action to your to-do list and storing your notes for future reference.
- **Move the dial time** - to ensure you focus on incremental progress against your objectives and create real value for your firm. It is crucial to allocate at least 30mins of your day towards this activity; this should be blocked out in your calendar to protect this time.

During this time, you should review your objectives as set by your line manager and challenge yourself to make one small action to try and make progress on your objective each day. Without allocating such time, the danger is that you can spend your day only on the urgent tasks that cross your desk, which means you will end up neglecting the critical tasks that create the most long-term value for your firm.

- **Weekly review** - sit down at the end of the week and review progress on your to-do list. Next week is the time to take care of initiatives that have stalled or ramp up specific tasks that need doing. Protect at this time. A title like "No meetings please" ought to do the trick. A weekly review ensures that you end the week on a positive note and don't return to the office on Monday with unfinished tasks. Key components of your weekly review include doing:

    1. Review the forthcoming meetings and check what preparation/actions need to be completed ahead of the meeting

    2. Review meetings from the past week and add any actions to your to-do list and follow up with any stakeholders on promised actions

    3. Try to clear your inbox to zero, do not let last week's emails greet you Monday morning.

- **Monthly review** - similar to the weekly review; however, this instead focuses your time on initiatives that span a few weeks and will be a valuable opportunity to check progress toward your objectives and prioritise specific initiatives similar to the weekly review. Focus at this time on reviewing your progress on your objectives, determining when your following performance review is and what steps you need to take to achieve your objectives ahead of these meetings. **[see CHAPTER 18]**

**Expert view**    William Walder, Head of Business Development
(London) at Latham Watkins, based in London:

*"Strategy and strategic thinking sound very C-suite. But the strategy doesn't need to be limited to the responsibility of executive-level managers within your firm. Strategy can be defined and executed closer to home, and it's simply about forming a plan to achieve a stated objective. For example, my strategy around career development and my focus in my role this year will be to build and maintain a stakeholder map to ensure I am in regular contact with key people. To me, strategy is about taking a step back from day to day, looking at where you want to be in a given time frame and then forming a plan to get there. Here are some practical thoughts on behaviours for strategic thinking:*

*Try not to tackle all the significant issues of the day, or you will find yourself getting lost in a futile attempt at boiling an ocean. You also need to think carefully about what's in your wheelhouse (as my American colleagues say) or what your role can effectively impact. For example, you would be correct in looking at technology and the digital agenda as a potential influence/impact on the business. Still, you may struggle to make it relevant to your area. Instead, pivot your thinking and consider if technology/digital will (or could) impact your practice area, your clients or the firm. We recently had a client request that required us to sift through large thousands and thousands of lines of data. By simply being aware of and conversant in the way AI tools work, we were able to apply AI to the problem, delivering a quick result with minimal effort and ultimately a satisfied client.*

*Find ways to extricate yourself from day-to-day life. Usually, this means carving out specific times outside of regular hours to take an elevated position and think about the business, which helps to change the scene. Sit in a coffee shop. Go to the meeting room. I often can be found taking a break in the office café on a Friday morning to reflect on the firm, my role, the strategy, or simply figuring out how to deal with challenges we have got coming up next week.*

*Use this time to be brutal with yourself. Be highly selective about what you allocate your time and energy to doing. Regularly ask yourself:*

- *Where can I realistically make an impact?*

- *What time do I have? How much time can I devote to this?*

- *What will make a difference to my role? Will it help me get promoted/ support annual review objectives?*

- *What are the points of friction? What's broken?*

*The strategy will change and develop with your career as the objectives will change by becoming more complex. Someone recently said to me, "as you get more senior, you think further ahead". I think this is true; your scope of thinking needs to change. But in general, the behaviour will primarily be the same, e.g. take a step back regularly and think about where you need to be and the tasks you are doing."*

## Pricing and commercial acumen

Due to the economic crisis, the professional services industry has undergone dramatic changes in recent years. The number of firms has grown to the point that they are now competing in a very homogeneous market offering similar services. Further, clients are more price-sensitive, and they expect delivery times to be shorter, as well as higher quality.

Consequently, you will no longer be able to simply describe what your firm does and how long it will take clients in your marketing or business development role. You must now consider the full impact of your service delivery. Are you solving the business problem? Maximising ROI? Can you add value over and above what competitors would do? Are there ways you can demonstrate this? Have you earned the trust of the potential client?

The answers to these questions could play a significant role in the price you can charge for your services. Learning how professional service firms use price as part of the 7Ps marketing mix will help you differentiate from the competition and move up in your firm.

## Expert view

Stuart J T Dodds, former Director of Global Pricing and Legal Project Management at Baker McKenzie and now co-founder and Principal of Positive Pricing, based in London:

*"Business Development and Marketing teams within the professional services industry have a pivotal role to play in driving and supporting greater pricing confidence. The key to this is 'be ready for the opportunity that lies ahead and focus on client value'. Ultimately this will drive your success.*

*Clients are increasingly seeking value and efficiency from their advisors - with that value coming at an appropriate (and for some, read lower) cost. Those of you regularly involved in client proposals, client relationship management and client feedback programmes will be all too aware of these messages.*

*The prevailing pricing model adopted within professional services (and legal especially) is still cost-driven rather than value-driven. Service price is affected by the input costs (i.e. our time), not the end value of the result to our client. In a value-based approach, we start with what our client is willing to pay, determine the actual value to our client, and then try to control our cost as much as possible to meet the price that most accurately reflects that value and is in line with what our client requires. Current pricing theory states that we should consider all three elements - our costs, our competitive market (which acts as a moderator to our price) and the value of the work to our ultimate client - all the time. In other words, the complete opposite of what many professional service firms do today.*

*You can summarise any product or service's perceived value using a simple equation - 'perceived value equals perceived benefits/perceived sacrifice'. We do this calculation every day, working out the potential benefit of a specific purchase compared to how much it will cost us and how much time it would take us to do (the 'sacrifice').*

*However, the ability to identify, build and generate value in the context of service can feel much less straightforward to explain. We need to recognise how we create and deliver value for our clients, communicate this value to them, and convince them that they must pay for the identified value. The Marketing team often holds excellent insights to share, such as the state of the current client relationship, likely competitors, and how to best craft (and rehearse!) any proposal.*

*Creating and delivering value for our clients should be our prerequisite. Frequent examples include mitigating a perceived or actual risk, generating additional revenue through the launch of a new product line or acquisition, or helping our clients decrease their overall costs or improve the general overall performance cash flow.*

*We add value by offering distinct to (and ideally better than ). The Marketing team plays a key role in communicating your firm value; you must do so in your client's language – the language of business – and in a way that is directly relevant to them.*

*Those who want to advance into senior roles within the Marketing team will require a greater understanding of what drives and influences profitability and exhibit strong commerciality.*

*They will need much stronger business development skills earlier in their career as they seek to differentiate their offering and value in an increasingly competitive marketplace (this, in turn, is supported and complemented by a strong pricing awareness and focus on value as above)."*

## Being strategic doesn't mean you forget to get your hands dirty

This chapter has focused on the importance of taking a more strategic focus to your role and how this will help advance your career and build stronger relationships with your internal stakeholders. At the same time, it is important to stress that as you move your career towards more senior roles, you regularly challenge yourself and those in your team by asking them, *"are you asking others to do something you are not prepared to do yourself"*.

---

## Expert view

Jeremy Ford, European Head of Marketing at Skadden, Arps, Slate, Meagher & Flom, based in London:

*"The 'transition from focusing on tactics to the more strategic side of our roles' is an interesting area. In recent years, I have been somewhat alarmed by candidates at all levels saying they want to focus on "strategy". The implication is that getting involved in the tactical work is somehow not valuable or deemed a necessary evil, whether working on pitches, directory submissions or maintenance of the CRM. I entirely disagree with this attitude.*

*Our ultimate goal is to be a trusted adviser to our stakeholders, guiding them on the best ways to help improve the level and breadth of business we receive from clients and utilise sophisticated communications channels to augment the firm's brand and its practices. These responsibilities are also what our partners have to focus on in addition to their legal work: reviewing/ writing pitches, making presentations, hosting roundtables, seminars and panels, reviewing and editing directory and award submissions, inviting their clients to events, writing content and so on.*

*For a marketing professional to think of themselves as above such responsibilities is the opposite of the role itself. The most successful marketers I know in the industry work shoulder-to-shoulder with their stakeholders. I am over-stating the point deliberately as I think this is the single most important message I can give anyone developing their career in professional services marketing. At the senior level, it is, of course, true that it's crucial to lead mid-to longer-term projects, which somewhat reduces the ability to be tactical. However, the critical point here is that your experience guides you in judging when/where to be tactical but not focusing on escaping getting one's fingernails dirty. You must never be "too posh to pitch"!"*

---

 **Key points to remember**

1. Ask yourself and others when planning and delivering marketing initiatives, "How does this help our clients?"

2. Ensure you understand your firm's strategy and review how your objectives and tasks align with this

3. Make a list of companies outside the industry that inspire you with novel ideas to create better marketing for your clients.

4. Gain further insight and develop relationships with your clients to generate and test your ideas. But do not lose sight of getting your hands dirty as you advance your career.

# 7

# Planning and delivery

*"Pause to find what's working, evaluate how to hard-wire success into ongoing transformation and teach the new ways"*
*—Laura Starita*

## Flexible and adaptive planning

When you receive your marketing budget for the year, do you find that you spend a great deal of time creating plans that everyone will not look at again? Or where is it so rigid that the minute a new trending issue becomes the focus, all other activities instantly feel obsolete?

As you are aware by now, professional service firms are notorious for creating complex three-year and annual plans that take a lot of time, input, and do not adapt to change as they are not flexible. Marketing plans can quickly become outdated especially when not updated, resulting in your firm being slow to market and thus losing relevance to your client's needs as your competition is faster. Therefore, it is vital to create a fluid plan regularly reviewed by key stakeholders and used as a roadmap for your marketing activity each year.

Big campaigns take a lot of resources - time, money, and people. Then when launched, they often fail to reach the intended objectives or the metrics are not reviewed enough. It is more advantageous to break down campaigns into smaller components that provide more immediate feedback from your clients on how your campaigns are performing. Have you ever focused your energy on creating a single anchor piece of marketing, such as a thought leadership report that is forgotten about soon after being released? Did it involve a significant focus over recent months? Use a fair chunk of your marketing budget?

Your clients face various macro-political trends and pressing challenges depending on the sectors in which they operate. Almost out of nowhere, some of these events, such as the coronavirus (COVID-19) outbreak, can scupper any current marketing priorities and plans you have in place.

Clients are busy, and we operate in a crowded market. Rather than focusing your attention on one overarching initiative that goes unnoticed for not creating enough engagement, it's better to do a few initiatives consistently well to improve your firm's brand, instead of focusing on implementing large infrequent marketing initiatives. Moving to more frequent marketing output will allow you to create more regular interaction with your clients, e.g. more concise client communication sent monthly or quarterly rather than annually.

As well as being flexible in your planning, it is essential to be adapting your marketing approach constantly. By analysing what is working and whether your activities contribute to growth, you can walk away from those activities that no longer deliver a return on investment (ROI). I have previously stopped marketing activities such as costly industry memberships and specific initiatives where results have stagnated. Because we have always done these activities, it does not mean it is an excuse to continue doing such activities in the future. **[see CHAPTER 8]**

Rather than being stuck in areas you have invested in already, your ability to adapt quickly to where clients need you will give you a competitive edge. To achieve long-term client growth, identify trends, areas that will impact clients, ways to communicate your services, and unique value proposition (USP) within these areas.

## In practice

Before the outbreak of COVID-19 globally, we had just created a three-year strategy for the Industrials sector at Eversheds Sutherland.

The plan set out a defined approach to extensive marketing activities and where we planned to invest our budget for the year. Yet when the pandemic arose, instantly, many of our ideas and budget items were no longer relevant as clients' needs and priorities shifted overnight.

Our team had to quickly respond to this change in strategy, identify new ways of marketing to our target audience, and focus on the critical messaging we wanted to communicate to our clients at a difficult time.

We focused on more consistent marketing focused on the client and measured everything to understand which activities were more relevant and received the most engagement from clients. When the market felt very crowded with numerous webinars and other digital activities going on, this was helpful in us staying "top of mind" with our clients and contacts.

These activities, such as regular weekly calls with clients and monthly technical workshops to work through a client's frequently asked questions, were more impactful than any other form of marketing we found in our discussions and monitoring client engagement.

If you can remain agile in planning and identify your client's future needs, you will be well-positioned to help your firm position itself more relevant to your clients than your competition.

**Expert view**  Peter Kane, Managing Director and Founder of The BD Consultancy and former Head of Business Development at Deloitte (South West England), based in Bristol:

*"Whether we love them or loathe them, annual strategic reviews are now largely obsolete. Our approach should involve creating a live and adaptable plan that crucial people can regularly engage with; to endorse, challenge and reimagine.*

*The future will continue to be a period of trial and experimentation. A hybrid work strategy is new to all of us. Regularly reviewing and adapting to what is working (and what is not) while maintaining fluent communication with clients and colleagues is crucial for success.*

*Also, to resume new client campaigns as if nothing has changed is ridiculous. We need to apply what we have learned about nuclear levels of speed, focus, technology and channel adoption to ensure our messages rise above the crowd.*

*Now is the time to demonstrate how flexible your firm truly is."*

## Identifying and responding to future client needs

Strategic thinking requires looking ahead. In your role, you must understand your clients to anticipate what issues may arise later, what challenges they may face, or how they might change in the future.

To detect future issues, focus on learning what clients care about. You can do this by understanding what macro trends affect the business and industry in which they operate. Subscribe to online publications, read books, listen to podcasts; however, you like to consume content and learn new things.

Client discovery is the best way to scope these, and execution is the best way to market them [see **CHAPTER 6**]. Often clients want information fast. That is not to say your 20-page technical briefing is not relevant, but you can deliver it later. Be sure your briefing is not your client's tenth within a week.

If your firm has been too slow to market an idea or project, you should never hesitate to axe it. Something that I frequently experience due to internal blockers and cost of delay, which we will cover in more detail later on [see **CHAPTER 8**]. If you have just developed an idea and subsequently discovered your competitors have already covered it. You must never be afraid to walk away mid-project if it saves you from producing something your clients have already received from your competitors.

**Expert view**  Rahul Gossain, Head of Marketing Communications & Delhi Region BD at Cyril Amarchand Mangaldas, based in Delhi:

*"Strategic behaviour is the cornerstone to achieving the desired marketing impact in complex matrix organisations like law firms and consulting firms. You must take on board the potential actions and reactions of a diverse set of internal and external stakeholders, including clients, policymakers, media, independent institutions across both domestic and international markets. Therefore, when making marketing decisions and carrying out marketing initiatives, you need to evaluate everything you do strategically.*

*Especially relevant in jurisdictions like India that restrict firms from actively seeking new business. Experience, historical context, ongoing stakeholder engagement, and diverse subject-matter knowledge equip you to effectively gauge the potential response of the stakeholders to any initiative. Strategic behaviours thus help carve out a broad framework to strategically approach marketing and strategic communications by ensuring an appropriate balance between strategic goals, outright impact, and potential risks associated with tactical approaches and innovation fundamental to engaging and effective marketing and communication.*

*Clients expect firms to provide cutting-edge advice, which would enable them to gain a competitive advantage or overcome challenges. Your role within the Marketing function is to effectively position and differentiate your firm.*

*It would help if you had a myriad knowledge of technical areas relating to your firm's service, evolving global trends, over and above marketing skills. Whilst you may find satisfaction in your role through testing the limits of creativity and innovation, lawyers often have the conservative technical driven approach to the market.*

*The real test for you in your role is to put aside individual preferences and respond in a way that aligns with your firm's objectives, strategy, and plans agreed with the leadership team."*

## Keep it simple

One of my lecturers repeatedly challenged us to adhere to this value when developing ideas during my marketing degree. We can sometimes have a great idea but then overthink it, adding more and more to it. We love overcomplicating things, and maybe it's because we're all perfectionists?

*"Perfection is achieved not when there is nothing more to add, but when there is nothing left to take away" - Antoine de Saint-Exupéry.*

Further on, I have set out an essential project planning framework that allows you to keep focused on the essential and overcomplicating ideas. It's okay to add elements as you go, but you should always come back to the objectives. What are you trying to accomplish? What is the easiest way to achieve this? In addition to keeping your efforts realistic, this value ensures you don't over promise or lose sight of the big picture.

Consider the most straightforward way you can complete your next task. Don't overcomplicate your approach. In the end, you'll be able to make it more presentable by adding details.

## Stop trying to be perfect

There is a difference between delivering quality and accurate work to stakeholders and being a perfectionist. The problem of being a perfectionist in a fast-paced environment with an ever-increasing list of tasks to complete is that it's inefficient. Perfectionism can lead you to believe that your decisions will fail, and stakeholders will criticise you if you decide that you did not make the correct decision or create something perfect.

In many cases, you may feel your internal stakeholders expect you to anticipate every possible outcome beforehand for your marketing initiatives to be successful. In reality, weighing every possible outcome and considering every detail is paralysing.

## Perfectionism - how to overcome it?

- **Don't spend more time and effort than you should on a task** - keeping it simple is a great way to prevent this from happening. Don't add unnecessary detail or complexity to a task. Often, this results in stakeholders becoming annoyed with you for spending too much time and not delivering the solution sooner. Scope stakeholder requirements and be clear about what's needed and when.

- **Stop procrastinating** - sometimes, it is easy to put things off or wait to find the perfect moment to accomplish a task. In reality, such an ideal moment rarely comes along, and therefore can delay initiatives from being completed on time, resulting in stakeholders asking for updates. Make progress today, and if a task overwhelms you from the start, break it down into smaller tasks and identify specific tasks that others can help you complete.

- **Focus on the big picture** - you must recognise the big picture; otherwise, your task may delay others from achieving their goals. Avoid getting caught up in the small details of delivering a project, such as making a PowerPoint deck look visually appealing when your audience is more concerned with the content.

Before your next initiative, ask yourself these questions:

- Out of all the stakeholder groups, which one or two would you least want to disappoint? In terms of this initiative, what is success to them?

- What decisions do I need to make to have the most significant impact on my key priorities?

- What action should I take today to move closer to my goal?

- What's the one task or action I can do that will make everything else easier or unnecessary?

- What are the best next steps based on what I know and the information I have at the moment?

- What is the worst thing that could happen? Is that likely to happen?

**Expert view**     Roy Sexton, Director of Marketing at Clark Hill Law and serves as the Legal Marketing Association (LMA) president-elect in 2022 and president in 2023, based in Detroit:

*"What I learned and experienced at the beginning of my career was that there is a connective tissue that runs from intentional strategy through effective execution and measurement onto external communications, community engagement, and colleague satisfaction.*

*In my subsequent roles, I've employed that philosophy. Attorneys, in particular, always wonder why "the marketing person" wants to ask questions about strategic direction and internal communications. Through the experience I had learned and implemented previously, I've successfully illustrated for them that success comes from a healthy culture. Clients want to work with a highly functioning and inclusive team, and those same clients are actively measuring law firms on that criterion for future work. Clients assume an attorney knows the law; they want to know whether or not the attorney is collaborative and engaging.*

*We are in a DIY digital marketplace, and those who provide compelling content – accessible, helpful, insightful, authentic – rule. In all of my marketing and communications roles, I have been a champion for translating the brand into a digestible narrative, with a heavy hand toward media relations, social media, and bespoke digital communications, like podcasting and webinars, and video. My theatre training has shaped my perspective throughout – be lean and resourceful and learn to read your external and internal audiences.*

*I've always invested in how brands translate internally and build a client-centric culture – are our language and context helping us engage with each other and those clients we serve? Your firm's brand is consistent across all stages of the client journey; however small the details are, for example, how someone answers the phone or an email, how welcoming our physical space may be, and how we interact as a team."*

## The most prepared person in the room

Most meetings fail because people are unprepared. The meeting organiser often does not think about what the meeting is for and what they want to achieve, wasting everyone's time and energy. Meetings do serve a purpose, however. They can be used for planning, collaborating, and agreeing to initiatives, specifically when groups are too busy to communicate via email.

For each meeting, determine what you want to get out of it, what you believe others will be interested in and identify any information gaps you need to fill to be clear on the agenda and expectations in terms of your contribution.

Before a meeting, you should carry out research. Being well-read about a topic likely to be discussed during a session is essential. If you're meeting with a particular client, make sure you research their business, their recent activities and anything else that may be helpful. If you're meeting a new partner, make sure you research their expertise, published work and any other information about them that would be useful. Read ahead of time as often as possible.

Since virtual meetings are becoming more common, it's also possible to research the call. If someone mentions a new development, you can examine it during the meeting, or if there is a client you have never heard of, you can visit their website instantly to find out more. One way to make yourself invaluable to specific stakeholders is by being well informed.

## In practice

Like you, I have far too many meetings and find that when I am jumping from meeting to meeting, I am ineffective, unprepared, and unable to contribute fully to each meeting if I do not have time to prepare for a meeting ahead.

One of the habits I have focused on implementing over the last year is to be more prepared ahead of any meeting I attend. I recommend you consider adopting this approach, ensuring you include meeting preparation as part of your weekly review, as covered previously.

Often, I feel I don't even have time to catch my breath when I have back-to-back calls and jump from one to the next. How can I be expected to be prepared to contribute meaningfully to each call? Scheduling time in my weekly schedule to prepare ahead of meetings allows me the necessary time to set aside my talking points/objectives for that meeting, rather than preparing ten minutes before. By preparing ahead, I can also store my meeting notes for easy reference in an appointment alongside the meeting, enabling me to grab them ahead of meetings quickly.

Ahead of the meetings, I now follow the below checklist to ensure I am well prepared to make the best use of my time in the meeting and meaningfully contribute to the discussion.

Are you prepared for your next meeting?

- Why is this meeting being held? Be sure to contact the meeting organiser ahead of time for an overview/agenda if there is none.

- Is your attendance essential, and what input do you need to provide clearly?

- Have you reviewed all pre-readings and requests in advance?

- Did you complete any tasks promised in a subsequent meeting?

- Have you reviewed and researched all the attendees?

- Identify desired outcomes and actionable follow-up tasks?

Another helpful idea is to keep a rolling agenda in your favourite note-taking tool. When you add discussion points to recurring meetings with key stakeholders such as your boss, this can include progress against your objectives, updates on work they have set you and other developments worth discussing regularly. You can add and delete items ahead of the call that you then share with them as an agent. You can then make sure you have all the input you need on various topics rather than trying to remember them afterwards. It is essential if you have busy stakeholders, as you need to take advantage of their time when you have it.

 **Key points to remember**

1. Avoid rigid marketing planning that cannot keep up with clients' evolving needs and prevent regular touchpoints from creating value for your clients.

2. Subscribe to resources to better understand your clients and their industry so you can anticipate their future needs

3. Focus on the essentials and keep it simple when planning and delivering marketing initiatives

4. Ensure you plan and put aside time to prepare for meetings effectively to ensure you are not wasting your time and others

# 8

# Results driven by data

*"Marketing without data is like driving with your eyes closed"*
*—Dan Zarrella*

## Validated Learning

You may have heard internal stakeholders say, *"This is how we did it for years,"* or *"This is best practice,"* but can you accuse your firm of becoming complacent and inert? Unless you can prove they no longer work, are too expensive or do not contribute meaningfully to the firm's objectives, you will often encounter resistance when attempting to eliminate such activities that previously seemed to work.

Trained advisors in the industry specialise in negotiation; they are concerned with facts. What steps can you take to circumvent resistance from your internal stakeholders so that they will accept your recommendations? The answer lies in a data-driven approach.

In your role you should develop marketing strategies based on data and return on investment (ROI) instead of overreliance on opinions and conventions to make decisions. This global pandemic has validated the value of these costly annual sponsorships to industry bodies and client conferences held in one specific location. To move past the statements above and towards more purposeful and relevant marketing for your firm, you must be able to identify and articulate what success looks like for your firm as a result of its marketing efforts.

You may not be able to track what part of your marketing efforts have resulted in actual revenue in the professional services industry because the purchasing process is more complex and prolonged than in other industries. Traditional marketing techniques like sponsorship, print advertising, public speaking, and networking are still largely unquantifiable marketing methods, making it difficult to quantify whether they have been successful. That's not to say they shouldn't be part of your marketing program, as the most successful firms often use a combination of traditional and modern online techniques to reach their audiences.

Where specific channels are unquantifiable, make them measurable through taking a more intelligent approach such as having a particular code on an advert, using a dedicated hyperlink or having the enquiries sent to a specific location.

## Expert view

Naomi Rendell, Marketing and Business Development Manager at Howes Percival, based in Cambridge:

*"Most marketers will be familiar with the famous saying, 'half the money I spend on advertising is wasted; the trouble is I don't know which half".
Fortunately, in the digital age, we are now in a position where we have more data than we know how to use effectively.*

*Digital marketing tools like Google Analytics mean we are spoilt for choice regarding metrics and KPIs, allowing us to identify precisely where we get the most ROI online.*

*But how do you measure offline marketing tactics? We often assume that ROI from more traditional marketing methods, such as print advertising, is difficult to measure, so we often neglect to do so.*

*Where digital campaigns offer more in-depth data, it is still very possible to track the effectiveness of offline campaigns and even bridge the gap* between traditional and digital marketing. Here are some ideas for how to measure your offline marketing:

- Direct your target audience to a custom landing page on your website – you can focus the page towards that audience and track how many people land on the site.

- Alternatively, direct your target audience to one point of contact – that person can then log how many enquiries they received during the campaign.

- Promotional codes – depending on your firm's brand and overall marketing strategy, adding a special offer to a print campaign allows you to track how many clients used that code (e.g. "quote 'X' for a free 30-minute call with one of our experts").

- Track traffic to your website before, during, and after your offline campaign – has there been an increase in traffic? Of course, correlation does not always equal causation, but this can help to indicate the campaign's effectiveness.

Finally, it's essential to factor in qualitative data when reviewing your online and offline marketing efforts. Ask your clients and contacts about their view of your brand in the market. Also, how visible you are and monitor how this changes over time.

As marketers in professional service firms, it is important to demonstrate ROI to stakeholders and use data to guide future marketing initiatives – even when a campaign's effectiveness seems impossible to track. As Galileo famously said, 'measure what is measurable and make measurable what is not so'."

It is vital in your role to ensure you are using the data to make informed decisions rather than being primarily led by the data. Your expertise and experience will help you to generate ideas and recommended approaches. The data will allow you to measure, adapt and respond to changes that help your firm strategically achieve its objectives.

As firms increasingly turn to digital marketing activities such as email marketing, webinars and social media, each of these offers different ways to measure whether your marketing efforts are helping your firm develop ROI.

## Marketing ROI - How do you calculate it?

- **Set goals** - be as specific as possible when defining success for your marketing campaign. Your objective might be to make clients aware of particular services you offer or to schedule a certain number of new meetings. The goal is to determine which metrics contribute most to revenue generation.

- **Measure and analyse the data** - once you have established your objectives, it is now time to measure and analyse different data sets to determine the success of your campaign. A digital-focused marketing method such as email marketing allows you to measure items such as how many people opened the email, clicked the link, unsubscribed, bounced, and shared it.

- **Determining success** - Account-based marketing (ABM) is becoming increasingly popular among firms, where you market to one or a few key client relationships and measure their engagement with your marketing efforts; for example, how many accepted your webinar invite? How many joined on the day? To measure the success of your client events, you should review the number of attendees it attracts, but more importantly, who attended and their importance in the client's organisation, the revenue a specific client generates annually, instructions from contact.

If you can clearly and concisely capture why something works or does not work, you can strategically advise partners on what marketing activities to focus on going forward. To find the answer to this, you need to pilot your concept.

## Key to Success - Piloting Ideas

Rather than launching a large campaign, firstly test your ideas on a few clients to get immediate feedback, as previously covered [see **CHAPTER 6**]. You avoid wasting resources e.g. time and money, when you test the interest from clients in your idea.

Testing your idea will help you determine if it is worthwhile and will it work? Before expanding your reach, where do you need to spend more money to get it right? It might sound basic, but this approach avoids you launching a initiative right away and hoping for the best.

It's crucial to work with your target audience to gather this feedback, so you can create content that ultimately delivers value to them.

## Defining success

Does your firm often focus on the what and when rather than the more important how and why?

When planning your next initiative, take the time to plan and prepare at the start of each task to ensure that you and stakeholders can visualise the direction and destination you anticipate heading in. You can then identify the specific steps to achieve your objectives and clarify why you are doing something. You would likely create something without taking the time to understand how such an idea would benefit clients.

I have provided the below marketing project framework template, available to download for free [see **INTRODUCTION**]. I have used it countless times and continue to use it, when putting together marketing plans, campaigns, white papers, and other materials. You can use this to outline the why and how for each of your marketing projects . It is also a helpful format to share with busy partners involved in the initiative since it clearly outlines the basics of the plan.

## Key Marketing Project Planning Considerations Framework

| | |
|---|---|
| **Project Name** | *Identify the project by its name* |
| **Project Lead(s)** | *List all key internal stakeholders involved in this project and their responsibilities. Identifying lead decision makers for each project.* |
| **Kick-off date** | *What will be the start date for this project?* |
| **Launch Date/Key Deadline** | *When will this go live / be sent to clients? It will help you stay accountable* |
| **Objective/Approach** | *What are you trying to achieve? (Link to your firm's overarching strategy and objectives)* |
| **Target audience** | *Who are you targeting, e.g., new contacts, existing clients, intermediaries, specific jurisdictions? Be clear about the target audience since this will help you determine which marketing channels to use to reach them.* |
| **Marketing Channels** | *Be everywhere your target audience will be looking for help! Sounds more straightforward than it is. Consider the best channels to position your firm and reach your intended target audience.* |
| **KPI/ROI Summary** | *How will you measure if you have hit your objectives? For example, what key clients do you want to engage with via this project? Opportunity created?* |

Establishing KPIs as part of the plan is essential, as it makes it easier to determine if you have been successful.

Increasingly, clients are turning to digital resources such as webinars, podcasts, and apps. Providing you with greater access to more data and tracking against KPIs that were previously impossible when using traditional marketing activities (e.g. print advertisements, direct mail and other methods).

To measure your progress towards reaching your objectives. Numerous marketing KPIs are available to measure depending on your firm's tools and processes.

To choose efficient marketing KPIs, it is first necessary to think about how your organisation and strategy fits into the big picture; this will help you to select marketing KPIs that match your company objectives and environment, for example, are:

- Achieving a higher level of revenue and reputation in a specific area
- Relationships with your key clients
- Developing new client opportunities
- Increasing your brand's presence in other countries

Digital marketing channel examples include:

- Social: followers; engagement; site visits; conversions
- SEO: impressions; site visit conversions; revenue
- PPC: impressions; click-through rate; conversions; cost per acquisition
- Email: delivery rate; open rate; click-through rate; conversion rate; revenue
- Referrals: referrals gained; site visits; conversions; revenue
- Content: content views/visits; bounce rate; content shares; conversions

Once you know what KPIs you're looking at and how to measure them, it's essential to review them frequently and track how they're changing over time.

Defining success, then replicating and scaling is the key to understanding what is working and maximising the potential of your marketing efforts. You will inevitably try new approaches that won't work; however, that is how you innovate and differentiate your firm from the competition.

**Expert view**     Si Marshall, Founder at TBD Marketing Ltd. The firm runs The Digital 100, which reviews the top 100 UK law firms digital marketing and ranks them against each other, based in Bristol:

*"Analysing data requires us to use a completely different side of our brain than producing creative work. It can be easy to fall into a pattern of just following your gut instinct instead of using data to help drive forward your strategy.*

*Being data agnostic, not knowing how to use the data or inform your marketing is the new glass ceiling for Marketing departments. The past 15 years have seen a rise in marketers becoming led by their desire to deliver, which is a purely tactical function and ignores the importance of having a strategy and then using data to demonstrate how we're proceeding against that strategy.*

*The only way to mitigate and navigate your way through the world of partners' opinions within firms is to use data to back up your marketing strategy. Data helps us make better-informed decisions.*

*So, it's vital to develop a balanced approach to using data and your gut instinct. If you favour one over the other, mistakes can occur, so combining both is the recipe for success. Understanding data helps to perform beneficial decisions within the business strategy. For marketers who are just setting out in their careers to learn how to use data, assemble the data you have and what the story is telling you, but don't forget your human side!*

*For any strategy to succeed, data and emotion need to be present. Great marketers are good at tapping into people's feelings, understanding there's an emotional element to buying and using this as part of what they're doing.*

*KPIs play an essential role within any marketing strategy, but they aren't everything. Over time, we better measure what good looks like; it's critical not to become too attached to them. Within each firm, KPIs will differ.*

But the most practical way of measuring them is to think of four simple top-line indicators for the four points in the Marketing journey (comms, marketing, BD, and CRM). These could be a share of the audience, marketing conversion rates, business development sales leading to an actual client, and how often existing clients refer you to new clients.

Each of these will guide you in the direction you need to take. For instance, if you are doing really well on marketing but not so well with retention, where are you going wrong? What do you need to introduce for it to change?

Then, all your lower level KPIs, such as likes on posts, attendees to events - which are also important - can be analysed when you know that you've got an issue in a particular area that is stemming the flow of your pipeline.

It's vital to look at the context of the data. Your data may show that your firm has gone down, for example, website rankings. But the bigger picture may reveal that everyone else's has gone down three times as much. Context is everything.

Approaching marketing with the balance of both emotion and data means that you can narrow your options and give you the ability to discard plans that won't work or are mismatched. In a busy world where opportunities seem infinite, it's a good starting place and can successfully help you plan your marketing investments.

A basic understanding of data is essential if a marketing strategy will thrive in the current environment. You don't have to know everything about how to manipulate data. Instead, start with getting comfortable knowing what data to collate, and then working with the data specialists who can present you what you need so that you can act on it."

## Kaizen

> *"The message of the Kaizen strategy is that not a day should go by without some kind of improvement being made somewhere in the company"*

> —MASAAKI IMAI

The beauty of hindsight lies in its clarity. Have you ever anticipated all scenarios in developing a marketing initiative, yet once you delivered it, you wished you had done things differently or anticipated problems better?

Kaizen, the Sino-Japanese word for improving continuously. To determine the success of an initiative and whether or not it was successful. It's essential to assess what lessons you have learnt and how you might proceed with the same initiative differently, having now had time to reflect on what went well and what should be improved.

It is crucial to develop feedback loops in this process. Analyse the feedback on performance, which can come from many sources, such as internal stakeholders or end-user clients. It is necessary to act on your feedback in the future. You'll add value to every active project when you have this mindset.

This type of behaviour will lead to you discovering new ideas, as you will be looking for ways to enhance them in the future.

Your role as a strategic leader demands that you continuously strive for new knowledge and ways to work, applying these lessons to future marketing initiatives. You should see every initiative as a learning opportunity. Still, too often, you will be so busy and likely will have moved onto your next task, that you miss the chance to learn the lessons from your initiative.

After each marketing initiative you are involved in, you must allow some time for everyone involved to transition from the hecticness of the initiative. Then arrange for a debrief meeting.

Try to keep the following in perspective when attending or to host a debrief meeting:

- Be thoughtful in evaluating performance, and your colleagues will have worked hard. Therefore you should avoid personal criticism and blame of others.
- Avoid discussing 'what should have happened, mainly what has occurred. Therefore you can only make suggestions for what could happen in the future.

- Remember that all marketing initiatives have a finite amount of resources (human and financial); keep the discussion practical rather than compare it to hypothetical scenarios, e.g. if we had double the budget for the project.
- Start with what worked well, and why did these parts thrive compared to other areas? By focusing on the positive first, you will ensure the overall tone of the meeting concentrates in the same way.

During the debrief, ensure that as a group, you evaluate internal performance (stakeholders engagement, investment from the core delivery team and other internal areas) and the external impact (e.g., client engagement, revenue generated, industry recognition and awards).

Ensure you collect and review any marketing data available [see **CHAPTER 8**]. Compare these results with original objectives you should have set out using the planning template covered previously.

After the debrief, you utilise the critical lessons in all future marketing initiatives, ensuring that you make gradual progress in whatever you do.

## In practice

Once I have settled in and built up my understanding of the new firm, I am then able to identify and recommend ideas, processes and initiatives I have done successfully at my previous firm and incorporate them at my new firm to help the firm grow. This is one of the benefits of working in the industry as firms are not the same in terms of strategy, expertise, and structure.

Be aware of doing the opposite and questioning why your new firm is doing certain activities, processes and initiatives. Suppose you identify areas that are underperforming or no longer relevant to clients. In that case, you need to be cautious in your approach as stakeholders might meet you with *"we have always done this"* or *"it is Partner X's brainchild, let's keep doing it"*. If there are activities that you identify as not contributing to your firm's growth, remember the importance of using logical data **[see CHAPTER 8]** to support your decision and, better yet, come up with ways to make their idea better.

## Winning business with data-driven insights

It is becoming increasingly difficult to grow revenue in the current client-centric market we operate in. Clients still scrutinise their spending in today's economy and are informed about prices, value, and competitive alternatives. As a result of these market dynamics, you need to develop insight-driven business development strategies that create more excellent value and efficiency.

Helping your firm move from a reactive to an insight-based approach will better attract new clients and retain existing ones. To achieve this, you must develop your knowledge and learn continuously in this area.

## Expert view    Alexander Low, Management Consultant at PA Consulting, based in London:

*"Seth Marrs from Forrester cited back in 2020 "Dynamic guided selling is a concept that is poised to become a reality in B2B sales organisation"*

*As part of Marketing, you need to start thinking, how do you use data to make more informed and better business decisions to achieve revenue outcomes for your firm? An excellent place to start is mapping the client journey and considering all the entry points that a new or existing client will begin and end.*

*A referral, inbound – which channel(s). Outbound – which channels e.g.email campaign, social and others. In an ideal world, you are then able to track this journey through your CRM, phone calls, emails and meetings, opportunity & value, pipeline value, forecasting, win/loss. Starting here will provide insight into which channels are most effective and not –*

*ideally with associated costs. Furthermore, it shows you the number of "touchpoints" or "cadences" to use SaaS tech sales vocabulary that a typical BD & Marketing process takes.*

*If you layer these data points with Finance data or matter data, you can make more informed decisions on where the "white space" is for similar clients, and therefore, what the next best course of action is to fill it – based on historical data you have. e.g. when a client instructs your firm on a matter relating to X, typically they go on to advise us on Y, in this time frame, and what needs to happen (from a "touchpoint" or "cadence" to get to that point.*

*Taking learnings from SaaS tech sales, one can consider augmenting your data with 3rd party data platforms, such as Bombora or Spikr. They provide intent data, to you Relsci, which gives you rich relationship capital insight over and above what platforms such as LinkedIn Sales Navigator (LISN should be in every BD professional's toolkit as standard). You can go even further if you wish and consider "psychographic segmentation" from platforms such as White Rabbit Intel.*

*For this to work seamlessly, it all needs to integrate into a single source of truth, typically your CRM system. The next layer in all of this is where is it appropriate to automate the process, such as CRM data capture – Introhive and LinkedIn Sales Navigator are your go-to for this. We then consider using AI to help guide decisions with nudges – Salesforce Einstein or Microsoft AI for Sales Insights. These can support everything from forecasting to assisting you with the following best action.*

*Next, this needs to be easy for stakeholders, especially in Outlook, where there is critical cross-platform integration. For example, Dynamics 365 email & calendar sync means the Lawyer can do a lot of CRM activity tracking without leaving Outlook.*

*Visualised data is essential to help internal decision-making based on the audience you are talking to internally. How will you surface this? Dashboards are the usual go-to, either through Power BI or Tableau. However, with the rise of AR/VR – jointly called Extended Reality or XR, there is some fascinating technology in this space. However, Just because it's there doesn't mean you should acquire it.*

*What does this all mean for BD & Marketing? Do we all need to become data scientists? No, but you do need to start taking a much more data-led approach to what you are doing-looking outside of the industry and understanding what other Sales & Marketing functions are doing. Requiring you to develop an understanding of your current technology stack's - I guarantee your firm is only using a fraction of the total capability of the MarTech you have in place, much like we only use a fraction of the ability of our smartphones.*

*Yes, this may sound hard. The reason being is that it challenges you and your firm's old processes and assumptions. Both for us and the way the professional services industry, on the whole, has typically "done" business. Those that choose to learn more about what the art of the possible is, understand where that can apply in your world will go on to do great things and advance their career to the top."*

---

 **Key points to remember**

1. Use data and track ROI to validate whether your marketing initiatives were successful.

2. Pilot your ideas before trying to launch too widely

3. When planning your next marketing initiative, use the "Key Project Planning Considerations Framework."

4. After each initiative, identify areas you could improve and implement next time.

# PART THREE

# Working together as a team

*'Talent wins games, but teamwork and intelligence wins championships'*
*—Michael Jordan.*

Besides improving your skills in developing and delivering work, it is also crucial to develop your ability to work well in a team to attain a shared goal. Throughout your career in the industry, you will be required to work with teams from other departments, not just on your own on initiatives. Each initiative usually brings a new set of colleagues along with it, too, so you'll have to show and consistently collaborate well with these colleagues to achieve the desired common objective and results.

Besides the Marketing team, you should realise that professional services firms have various people working in different roles, each with other objectives. It's crucial to deliver initiatives, build allies, and grow your reputation internally to manage relationships.

Working effectively across departments, offices, and jurisdictions is critical for firms. Therefore, Marketing teams must also work seamlessly together in a consistent manner. Knowledge, necessary information, and resources need to be shared. Client-centric Marketing teams will help their firms shine above the competition.

Ultimately, working well in teams will help you progress and increase your chances of receiving internal career opportunities. It is difficult to know everyone in a large firm, so getting this right is essential.

The key to this is developing your brand internally and establishing expert power that demonstrates your leadership characteristics. It's possible to succeed based on what you know and what you can contribute rather than relying solely on your titular power.

This section will provide insight and guidance on successfully delivering initiatives, managing your colleagues' expectations, and identifying the best processes and resources. It also prepares you for when you step up into a more senior role where you have to manage a team toward a specific objective.

# 9

# Collaboration

*"If everyone is moving forward together, then success takes care of itself"*
*—Henry Ford*

## Centred on the client

Working in a large firm with various Marketing teams can make it hard to avoid operating in a silo with long chains of commands to follow. Therefore, it is all the more critical that you collaborate consistently with colleagues and other teams to provide a client-focused and joined-up approach in your role to counteract these inefficiencies.

Be sure to be in frequent contact with colleagues in different parts of the Marketing team avoiding knowledge hoarding and to exchange information, identifying opportunities for collaboration, and sharing knowledge.

For professional services firms, silos within the Marketing team are a growing pain. The executive leadership and management team in marketing must prepare and equip their teams with the necessary mindset to break these harmful and destructive barriers. It is common in marketing for specific teams to have conflicting objectives, leading to siloed information and reluctance to share information across groups. Here are a few common symptoms:

- Teams lack relationships with each other.
- Duplication of tasks

- A broad group of people cannot easily access information.
- "Reinventing the wheel" duplicates a primary method created previously.
- Lack of ownership on initiatives, "not my job" mentality
- Team rivalry and turf wars
- Hoarding of knowledge

## Breaking down marketing silos

Although mentioned that senior leadership should break down silos in your firm, there are steps you can take in your current role to eliminate silo-like behaviour. When it comes to developing greater collaboration with the teams you work with, the only thing you can control is your behaviour and how you work.

Developing the following behaviours regarding communication and collaboration yourself will set an example and likely influence positive behaviour from others.

1. **Connect with your colleagues** - make an effort to build relationships across the Marketing team, focus on building your understanding of your colleagues' expertise and their priorities. Helping you identify what information and ideas you should share and work together. When new members join the team, reach out to introduce yourself as early as possible. Ensuring that they know what you are focused on builds a collaborative relationship straight from the get-go. With firms moving to a hybrid way of working with various teams working remotely from one another, this has become vital.

2. **Ask, ask, ask** - to correct unwanted behaviour; you must first build awareness that such behaviour is counterproductive. Examples typically relate to you not being copied on essential emails or consulted on something that sits within your responsibility. If you don't approach the person to ensure they share this information

in the future, you will continue to be frustrated when not sent information that is relevant to your priorities. You must reach out, such as:

> *"Hey Stephanie, I noticed you mentioned X; you would be interested to know; I'm focusing on X also. Would it be useful if you could share any updates on X with me in the future, and I will do the same with you".*

Consider sitting down with Stephanie to understand why she is focused on X and see areas to work together.

3. **Share information** - if you come across information you consider relevant to other teams in marketing, ensure you are actively sharing this, whenever you come across them. As well as establishing your reputation as a team player, you are also likely to receive reciprocity when exchanging information in the future on specific topics.

4. **Don't reinvent the wheel** - Check with various teams for existing ideas or initiatives that can be reused or used as a starting point before creating new ones, whether it be a template or know-how on how to deliver a webinar or a process. As you become more senior and experienced in handling a wide variety of initiatives, you can identify what to repurpose for new marketing and business development opportunities, e.g. take successful client targeting efforts to other clients facing similar legal needs.

5. **Try to be as helpful as possible** - this will be covered in more detail later in this chapter, but remember that marketing is a team with the same objectives. In this case, you don't ignore or tell your colleagues that "it's not your job" when asked for assistance. If you can help with the task, be clear on what you can contribute, avoid taking on ownership for the task and seek to understand what you can specifically contribute that will help them. On the other hand, if it is something for which you are not an expert or responsible, try to point them in the right direction.

## Expert view

Kristel van den Elzen, Senior International Marketing & BD Manager at DLA Piper, based in Amsterdam:

*"Senior stakeholders in the Marketing team are used to receiving quick answers, other marketing colleagues that need input, teams seeking collaboration across departments – your mailbox can quickly take over your professional life. You can often feel like you need to choose, but the good thing is it's usually not a matter of yes or no; it's a matter of when.*

*First, identify the most critical stakeholders to keep happy across the Marketing team. That includes others besides your manager; which senior stakeholders and other managers have influential power, for instance? Ensure you pick up their requests as a priority always.*

*For others, prioritise accordingly. The most important thing is acknowledging receipt and providing an estimated lead time for a response – keeping people informed and helping them meet their deadlines is crucial to the Marketing team collaborating and you progressing your career.*

*Also, remember that you don't have to answer every group email. Colleagues asking for best practices, templates, and specific information are typical examples; unless you have something helpful worth sharing, this is an easy win that will get you credit and build trust with the colleague. If not, don't. You'll end up being that helpful colleague that never has time for their projects."*

## Avoid knowledge hoarding

A culture of information silos often creeps into professional service firms, especially in larger firms, where different teams have varying priorities. When information silos surround teams, it is hard for you and your colleagues to keep up with what is happening outside their bubble.

Influencing knowledge hoarders rather than battling them is the key to combating them. The most important thing you can do, is to prevent resistance in the first place by emphasising the mutual benefits of knowledge sharing and by your behaviour.

Make sure you share anything you develop that would benefit others, whether it is a template, a format for an event, or another kind of activity that can be replicated. They might not have any use for it. Siloed teams are prone to hoarding knowledge, but getting into the habit will demonstrate to others that you are someone that has the team's best interests in mind.

So when you next develop something you are proud of and benefit others, forward it to that person.

Share things related to a colleague's area, such as new developments in the sector or news about competitors. It can be a quick LinkedIn message or email with a link, like, *"Hey Tom, I found this that might be of interest to you."*

Learn to let go of knowledge hoarding frustration. It is often difficult to have visibility into everything going on across firms, so instead of getting frustrated when you finally find out someone sent an email weeks ago and you were not aware of it, let it go. Sometimes in Marketing, you will feel like you need to know everything and have a 360-degree view and control of everything going on at any one time, but instead, try to focus on what you can realistically control. A hard lesson I have only just recently learnt in my career.

Partners expect Marketing to know what each other is doing in a joined-up manner. When the team loses trust and appears uncoordinated, this reflects poorly on internal stakeholders. As Marketing becomes more remote, sharing information and being connected with your colleagues will become increasingly important to you thriving in your role and the function as a team.

## Group decision making

In your role, when faced with a business problem to solve, consider who and how best to bring it to a group to analyse the situation and evaluate the best solution collectively. There are statistical reasons why groups can improve decisions, as follows:

- Groups increase the sample size of experience, and the diverse backgrounds and knowledge of different members increase the group's data. As a result, group discussion can amount to a "consider the opposite" simulation.
- You can improve forecasts and predictions by averaging the estimations of the different group members. The predictions of various team members can be contrasted and averaged out to arrive at a more reliable estimate.

## Learning from others

Throughout your career, you will work with many colleagues in the Marketing team who have different expertise and experience than your own. No matter how senior you become, you can always learn from the experiences and backgrounds of others in the team. When you acknowledge this and invest your time in allowing others to share it with you, you will understand the various issues that may arise in the future and bring them into situations where you need their support.

**Expert view** Andrew Katznelson, Director of Business Development at ReedSmith, based in New York:

*"Marketing, particularly at global firms, often involves long hours spent on intensive work and allocating so much energy to navigating internal politics and silos. This atmosphere does not always lend itself to the variety of perspectives that are useful for actual career development. It would help if you created networking opportunities for yourself within your firm.*

*Joining legal marketing groups and associations are essential for your external brand building. Still, maintaining a personal network of internal contacts can help supplement the insight you bring to your role. Put together casual gatherings of marketing peers - in-person or on Zoom - to have regular conversations about the work challenges you face and share success stories, providing access to best practices you can use in your role.*

*Inside your firm, be sure to build relationships with stakeholders outside of the Marketing department, including the pricing, knowledge management, legal operations, recruiting, and IT teams, to better appreciate the roles they play in forwarding the firm's strategic growth.*

*All of this provides different perspectives that help you break through the blinders you may inadvertently have from the everyday work you do in your current role. Expanding your network educates, empowers and enables you to add even more value to your current position."*

## Winning as a team

Due to an overly competitive culture and different teams focused on other objectives. You must understand that your marketing colleagues have the same end-in-mind objectives - the growth of long-term sustainable profit for the firm.

It's essential to be aware of where colleagues need information or your help on initiatives that are vital to the firm as a member of the Marketing team, e.g., a report for the firm's Executive committee, so delaying the sending of it will reflect poorly on the Marketing department as a whole.

As mentioned previously, you should try to help colleagues whenever possible and add value where you can by providing input and support. As a result, you create "relationship currency" that you can use when you need help from that person in the future.

Since many of the relationships between the Marketing function and internal advisors are built on perception and excellent service, contributing to the team's reputation and perceived performance will benefit the function.

The Marketing team as a collective must be protected and championed. Structured into different teams, each team aims to increase revenue and take market share from the competition.

It's easy to blame or badmouth your marketing colleagues when things move slowly or make errors on something that an internal client notices. Make sure you defend confrontations regularly and highlight specific achievements the Marketing team has made to your internal stakeholders. Managing the Marketing team's internal reputation is key to being recognised and rewarded by critical stakeholders in the business.

**Expert view**     Heidi K. Gardner, PhD, Distinguished Fellow at Harvard Law School and Faculty Chair of the school's Accelerated Leadership Program, based in Boston:

*"Over the last 15 years, we interviewed executive teams from fintech and agtech start-ups to global giants in financial services, biotech, and telecoms, to NASA, NGOs, and higher education institutions. Successful leaders in all sectors have one thing in common: they recognise that creating a working environment that embraces diverse experience and is rich with opportunity leads to innovative and results-driven solutions. Smart Collaboration Accelerator, a psychometric tool, was based on a decade of Harvard-backed research. We developed the Accelerator to help teams understand their behavioural tendencies and use them to achieve the business and talent-related benefits of Smart Collaboration.*

*Engaging in Smart Collaboration at every step along your professional path will serve you at all stages of your career. Early in your career, focus your energy on developing a reputation not only as a specialist in your field but someone who possesses a skill set that transcends any specific vocation. Throughout your career, seek out mentors from whom you can learn more than industry knowledge. Find - and emulate - leaders who understand how to invite and leverage the expertise and experience of everyone on their team.*

*As your career evolves into leadership roles, don't lose sight of the importance of promoting Smart Collaboration behaviours. Foster an environment that encourages - all, no matter how basic - questions and encourages constructive debate about proposed solutions. Connect with everyone in the Marketing team, regardless of their role or place in your firm's "hierarchy." Support every team member in exploring how they work best and discovering what tasks are of interest to their strengths, strengthening the team.*

*My Washington Post Best-seller Smart Collaboration: How Professionals and Their Firms Succeed by Breaking Down Silos revealed research specifically for the professional services sector. For the follow-up book Smarter Collaboration (Harvard Business Press 2022), co-authored with fintech strategic powerhouse Ivan Matviak, we interviewed executive teams from businesses worldwide. While we heard about new approaches and productive ways leaders have been navigating supply and demand issues and remote working challenges, embedding Smart Collaboration has been the constant interlaced strategy.*

*Smart Collaboration will empower you throughout your career. Understanding your strengths and, as a leader, leveraging everyone's experience and knowledge allows the team to unveil superior solutions, retains talent, and increases client satisfaction and revenue."*

## Building trust with your colleagues in marketing

Your colleagues are your 'relationship currency', generated by the investments you make with them. Your ability to advance your career is directly related to how others judge you, which is influenced by your relationship with them.

Your interactions with others should always be positive and helpful. If you do this, you will develop a reputation as a person others like to work with, and they will never have a negative comment about you. As part of your appraisal process, you should ask colleagues and stakeholders for feedback from various perspectives.

Be aware that your behaviour can harm your team when you are busy. Everyone does it, whether coming across as short, looking grumpy (when you are stressed), or not staying on top of the email, causing delays for others on the team. Ask three colleagues you regularly work with if they know things you do that are different from your usual behaviour when busy. You can build your awareness and stop this behaviour when you are busy.

The Marketing team will grow as your company grows. You should reach out to new team members to welcome them and offer to help them onboard to help them settle in and introduce them to the wider team. Do you remember your own experience of joining your firm? What things helped your onboarding process? What did you wish someone had told you? Assisting a colleague to settle in is not only the right thing to do, but actually, this might be someone with whom you may need to work closely in the future, so it is well worth your time developing a close relationship from the beginning.

---

**Expert view**  Gina F. Rubel, Esq., Founder and CEO, Furia Rubel Communications, Inc., is based in Pennsylvania:

---

*"In the age of work and message overload, your team members and stakeholders find themselves over-extended and over-scheduled, drowning in a sea of virtual or in-person meetings, emails, social media messages, texts, voicemails and snail mail, all of which require attention. Tasks often get pushed to the back burner, buried or forgotten. When your boss' or stakeholders workload or lack of responsiveness starts to affect*

*the delivery of your work product, it is time for you to manage up. Requires you to work with others you rely on and report to enhance relationships and improve workflow and productivity.*

*As a valued member of your firm, you must proactively address needs, provide friendly reminders, and offer suggestions when necessary. While managing up requires you to be proactive and "nudge" others, do it positively. It helps to understand others' workload, obligations, habits and preferences. You also should anticipate their needs, consider the timing of your request, be specific about the time within which you need a response (don't just say "end of the day;" say "tomorrow, DATE, at XYZ time"). Do what you can to lighten the load. When you manage up effectively, you will benefit because your relationship with your teammates and clients affect your ability to do your job successfully.*

*As someone who has been managing stakeholders and a team of public relations and marketing professionals at Furia Rubel Communications for more than 20 years, I appreciate it when members of our team manage up – and they're pretty good at it too."*

## Giving feedback

In your business, you will often collaborate with many different people. Often overlooked, but the key to building trusted relationships is gathering regular feedback and improving your way of working in the future. It is also crucial to recognise your colleagues' achievements and contributions regularly. Many of us thrive when we feel appreciated.

If you regularly work with individuals in the team, telling them what they do well and areas to improve on next time can be a compelling way of changing unwanted behaviours and encouraging the behaviour you want to see more of when you work together in the future.

Provide feedback regularly to others and recognise their contributions. Whenever you receive praise for a project (remember it was likely a team effort), copy the individual or identify their line manager and send a positive message. As a result, you often build further "relationship currency" with that individual.

Performance reviews might take place quarterly or annually, depending on your firm. Request feedback by asking when their next one is and asking that they remind you. By doing this, you build strong relationships with your colleagues and show your commitment to a team-based approach.

## Be specific with your praise

When praising your colleagues, avoid giving unspecific credit and expect it to motivate them. Instead, relate the praise to something specific they did well, ideally shortly after they did it.

Praising an employee for the sake of it won't come across as genuine; they need to know what they've done well. This way, your praise will be more authentic and will encourage that person to continue doing the specific behaviour or task; that is why you are praising them in the first place.

## Build a wider perspective

In your role, you have likely developed a strong relationship with other colleagues in the Marketing team; the danger is that your career can become siloed in the Marketing department alone.

In your role, you will often work with different functions outside of Marketing, e.g. IT, finance, HR, and others. To perform your role fully and collaborate effectively. While you don't need to know the technical details of these areas, understanding how each department functions and how they support the firm and most importantly can benefit you in your position, to deliver your objectives.

## Expert view

Rebecca Wright, Director, Global Head of Client & Market Development (Global Financial Markets) at Clifford

*"Something I feel passionately about is balance within my team and the relative importance of everyone's contribution. As a team sports enthusiast, I can say with some degree of certainty that you won't always win just because of one or two star players. When everyone in the team is pulling in the same direction, each individual has a clear understanding of how they contribute to the whole, recognising each other's strengths and weaknesses so that when you compliment and help each other, your chances of success are far higher.*

*Whilst your role is to bring that "market" perspective, I've always thought about the lawyers I work with as our internal clients. From the reception desk to the print room, all the way up to the Managing Partner, we are all part of the customer journey for our internal and external clients somehow. Understanding your role, the value of your contribution and finding ways you can continuously evolve and adapt is as much the key to success on the sports field as it is in the law firm.*

*I received feedback early in my career that I "asked the right questions". I always look for candidates/teammates with what I call a "curious mind", which I would define as a desire to understand and engage, whether with the task at hand, the team or the wider business. It's about arming yourself with information to challenge your understanding, which helps you make good decisions.*

*When I think about "stepping up" as a leader, I honestly don't feel it is that different to my role within the team. Whilst it is my job to make sure everyone knows their role and to hold people accountable, we can recognise each other's contributions and champion our collective successes at any level. Being part of a team is about supporting each other, being prepared to walk in the shoes of any one of my fellow team members when they need my support, having empathy and giving each other the platform we need to succeed."*

---

 **Key points to remember**

1.  Silos can be difficult to breakdown in firms, but your behaviour is the only behaviour you can control

2.  Learn to let go of knowledge hoarding and try to know everything

3.  Make sure your interactions with colleagues on the Marketing team are always positive and helpful.

4.  Provide feedback regularly to others and recognise their contributions

# 10

# Performing effectively

*"Give me six hours to chop down a tree and I will spend the first*
*four sharpening the axe"*
*—Abraham Lincoln*

The pressure to perform efficiently can come from many different stakeholders across your firm; it might be your line manager who wants everything yesterday or a senior stakeholder who wants everyone in marketing to develop more in less time.

To avoid falling into the trap of busyness, you are required to work smarter through managing your own time to focus on the right priorities, responding to new requests, and understanding what you need to contribute to. Planning initiatives with multiple moving parts and people to ensure you deliver on your objectives and your stakeholders' specific initiatives holds you accountable.

To advance your career and demonstrate to senior stakeholders, you can perform effectively in your role.

## Say "no" without fear!

Protecting your time can often be the most challenging but effective habit to develop. Being confident and managing new work requests becomes imperative if you are overworked and behind on critical initiatives. Maintaining your peer status and a healthy relationship is your primary objective when saying "no" to a colleague or stakeholder.

Often high achievers fall into this category and end up taking on more than they can realistically handle, and they default to responding, *"yes, I can do that!"*. Learning when to say *"no"* and tactfully is vital for conserving valuable time and energy. Don't take on more work than you can manage. There is no benefit to you, the person asking, or the firm.

Your hesitation in saying "no" is natural since you want to maintain relationships with stakeholders. But guarding your time is not the same as refusing to help. If providing your input is crucial, you don't have to spend an hour in a meeting when a quick call or email is enough to maintain the relationship without focusing too much time on this request. Later on, we'll talk about this in greater detail.

You will inevitably have to handle a few requests from senior stakeholders or your boss. Just suck it up and do it, these are your VIP stakeholders. Sometimes, though, managing expectations with others is necessary, and you are not uncooperative by saying no. To develop your career prospects, you must realise that you only have a limited amount of time to accomplish meaningful work every day. When you respectfully decline, you ensure that your everyday schedule gives your own work greater priority to focus on these tasks.

It is essential to develop your ability to manage your senior stakeholders effectively; this is a skill set you will need to hone to thrive in a senior position.

## The emphatic way to say "no", examples:

1. *"I am willing to work with you on X, but I am currently working on several urgent initiatives that will tie me up until Y. Could we pick this up then, so I can give it the attention it needs to be successful? Thank you."*

2. *"I would be pleased to support you on X, however (Insert important stakeholder) asked me to work on Z, so I cannot take on additional responsibilities at this time."*

3.  *"Yes, I can work on X. I'm currently working on Y and Z; what should I reduce in priority?"*
4.  *"I can't do [request], but X in the Marketing team might be better placed to help, let me check with them and come back to you."*

## Clearly define your role and your input on each task

As part of the Marketing team, do you tend to be overly eager to take on new requests, whether those tend to come from the Marketing team or internal stakeholders? Do you often find yourself trying to please stakeholders internally by responding to new requests without taking the time to understand the rationale behind them? This behaviour will increase your workload that can detract you from your primary priorities. Therefore, it is critical that you ruthlessly prioritise requests according to the objectives for which you are rewarded and measured.

It is essential to clarify what you need to contribute to colleagues and internal stakeholders, whether information, a review of something or a commitment to provide more support.

Knowing what you will be responsible for will allow you to prioritise ruthlessly. You can use scoping to understand your role in the initiative and the required inputs.

If you want to succeed, you must understand:

- "What does success look like for the initiative?"
- "What are the key marketing initiatives that map to those objectives?"
- "How long will it take you to complete those initiatives."
- "What resources will you need and have available?".
- "How do you see my role contributing to this?".

Next, become accustomed to saying "no" to tasks that are not urgent or crucial, as covered above.

> ## In practice
>
> When I made the step up as a manager, I thought the best way to demonstrate competence was to be "proactive" at all times and "own" initiatives, which meant I often ended up owning every new request which came my way. Resulting in me quickly overstretching myself over various marketing initiatives, each competing for my time. I made this mistake as my mindset still worked like it did when I was a Marketing Executive, taking on every new request from inception to completion.
>
> The CMO at the time saw me doing this and advised me to change my approach from always proactively owning these types of requests. Instead, he advised me to "pause" and to understand what was requested and required from me before jumping into action; I later realised these are two separate things. Implementing this allowed me to focus on inputting and providing only the essentials rather than becoming accountable for completing the initiative.

## Blockers and the Cost of Delay

"Blockers" is anything that completely prevents progress from occurring within a project. Your firm comprises of various individuals and teams, each with limited resources available and conflicting priorities.

Whether it is your internal stakeholders, you need to sign off an initiative, receive technical input from a partner or issues with resources in other teams, such as a design team unable to complete the project in time. These are all frequent examples of where you might experience "blockers" that can delay your initiatives and, ultimately, your progress on your objectives.

Thus, you will need to plan, develop, and launch initiatives most effectively.

"*Plans are nothing, planning is everything*," Eisenhower said. Plan the potential delays ("cost of delay") and how they will impact the timeline you are trying to achieve. Being fluid includes assessing and identifying ways to avoid delays. Using the following approaches will help you keep progressing with your current initiatives:

- **Use "buffers" when planning the timeline for your project** - this is where you allocate extra time for people who are busy/will likely ask for an extension to meet specific deadlines. This way, you can offer an extension and still be on course to achieve your deadlines.

- **Avoid single points of failure** - you should not rely on a single person to help you achieve the desired outcome on a marketing initiative. Most of the stakeholders you work with are extremely busy, so getting support on initiatives may be difficult. As part of the planning process, it is essential to identify alternative sources of support or multiple contacts; this will help when those involved get busy and cannot give you what you need. Furthermore, we will discuss what accountability traps are later on and how to do this in more detail by leveraging incentives to incentivise busy workers to prioritise their initiatives.

- **Input/capacity** - some internal stakeholders are busy and unable to provide feedback on marketing initiatives. A lot of the time, the success of your initiative is heavily dependent on the approval and input of busy stakeholders. Improve how you plan and manage initiatives by:
  - Limiting the number of stakeholders to just 1-2 eliminates the need for committees to vote on decisions.
  - If you rely too heavily on the same stakeholders for all your marketing initiatives, you will be competing with your other projects where they are working on them with you.
  - Before beginning a project, verify an individual's capacity, and if they do not have it, ask them who is on their team or a peer they know who can help you with it.

- **Establish time-bound deadlines** - When dealing with fast-paced initiatives with multiple stakeholders, delays will inevitably occur, and final hurdles to overcome. It would be best if you created unmovable deadlines that act as ultimatums to achieve the desired outcome of your project to avoid unnecessary delays and other stakeholders getting frustrated with slow progress. The message might be something like, *"Hi Craig, I am just waiting on your input into the report; if we don't get it by next Monday, we'll continue without your section and launch to avoid further delay"*. Either way, the project will move forward, and Craig may end up giving you the support you need sooner rather than later.

Understanding how to deliver marketing initiatives is crucial to your advancement to more senior roles, as you will be required to coordinate with the team to provide these initiatives. It is essential to know where help is needed to be on schedule. If you anticipate them early on, you can avoid blockers and be prepared to speak to team members if problems arise.

## Organising initiatives according to priority

You're almost certainly juggling a variety of marketing initiatives at any given time. Managing multiple initiatives at any one time requires you to determine the order in which they should be implemented and identify the obstacles blocking their successful execution. Prioritise them and quantify the delays that result from selecting one over the other.

1. Comparing the different marketing initiatives, what each involves, i.e. time commitment, involvement of other stakeholders and resources. If I completed such initiatives, what kind of results would they achieve? What was the goal of this project?

2. Assess the impact of ordering initiatives by priority on a company's cost of delay, i.e., which marketing initiatives will become less relevant to clients as time passes if not prioritised? Is it more time-sensitive?

## Assembled Teams

Protecting your time requires saying "no," as already mentioned. In addition to this, to ensure you manage new requests and help move your tasks along, look at opportunities to outsource work to others in the Marketing team and other internal teams.

Make sure you know all the expertise and resources available to you in your firm. Determine specific areas you can outsource to these functions as part of your initiatives. In larger firms you likely have access to a wider range of multidisciplinary professionals, so you'll want to leverage their expertise and work closely with the following teams: research, design, audio/visual, and digital to complete tasks.

It might be that you are often reluctant to utilise others because you want to control every aspect of your work. You believe you have the necessary domain knowledge that others don't have for you to trust them to carry out the task to the standard you often do. Then identify the tasks only you can do.

For example, if you attended a meeting and needed to research a client discussed, you could outsource this to your research team. You will also want to provide this client with a capability statement, and the design department can create a template for you. After the call, you can send the advisor a blank Word document to input the information. When you do this right, your role in this task is to bring it all together and package it, ready to follow up with those on the call.

At any given time, you are likely working on multiple initiatives. You can manage various initiatives efficiently by utilising this approach. Allowing others to accomplish specific tasks and trusting others is key to delivering initiatives effectively.

## Delegating and outsourcing tasks

When you can delegate a task, try to determine whether the teams have the expertise and knowledge required to maintain the high standards you set.

- **Focus on what you do best** - identify your strengths that contribute to your firm's success. These are the tasks you should keep doing.
- **Consider outsourcing the rest of the tasks** - the ones you are less skilled or those that others can do more readily are the ones you should consider outsourcing.
- **Invest in others** - If you move up the ranks to managerial roles, you will have to delegate some tasks that you are very good at to others. You cannot assume it will be a smooth transition if you leave the method to others to guess. Invest time in sharing your knowledge with them and keeping in touch to see where they need guidance. By doing so, you can remain involved and later hand these tasks over to others.

## Self-care to avoid burnout

Since this book promotes career advancement through hard work and training, it is crucial to ensure that you do this in a sustainable way. Those who try to achieve a high level of performance consistently often become burnt out. COVID-19 has spotlighted the importance of our mental, physical, and emotional wellbeing.

Too often, junior professionals put in too many hours, refusing to take annual leave, failing to set limits with demanding stakeholders, and neglecting their physical wellbeing until they burn out entirely because they fail to realise the importance of self-care.

I have put in long hours and avoided annual leave throughout my career, and it's a sign that I am a hard worker and productive worker. However, this is an outdated way of working, and it has been better to focus on being more efficient with my time to achieve the same desired results.

Burnout makes you no use to anyone. You will likely be unable to maintain this performance forever as you do not want to disappoint your boss or stakeholders.

Our working patterns have changed since COVID-19 interrupted our work routines. We continue to create new pandemic-induced habits that are unsustainable, whether it be managing our time ineffectively, speaking on virtual calls all day without breaks, or not getting fresh air and sunlight.

Remember your career is "it's a marathon, not a sprint".

 **Key points to remember**

1. Protect your time by saying "no" emphatically

1. Clarify what you specifically need to contribute on when you receive new requests

1. Identify blockers and plan for potential delays in your marketing initiatives.

1. Outsource specific tasks to others to accomplish more

# 11

# Generating ideas

*"The value of an idea lies in the using of it"*
*—Thomas Edison*

## How do you get others on board with your ideas?

The need to gain buy-in and approval to reach an inevitable outcome is ever-present in professional service firms. Making a change happen or bringing your ideas to market in your organisation depends on getting buy-in. This is not a straightforward process since stakeholders have different objectives, compensation packages and are motivated differently. The best ideas you come up with will never progress further unless you get support from people at all levels within your firm.

If you often struggle to get buy-in from key stakeholders in your firm, this might be down to your approach. Do you continually develop your ideas in isolation and then attempt to sell the idea to yourself and then with others? You then create an appropriate response to each objection stakeholders raise and defend your ideas.

Instead, try to obtain buy-in through a more collaborative approach: invite discussion and debate, and ensure everyone has the opportunity to contribute, resulting in all being more invested in the idea and outcome of an initiative once launched.

## Gaining trust and cooperation from stakeholders

- Getting buy-in requires putting your ideas in draft form and demonstrating how they will help the firm achieve its objectives. Use the 'Key marketing Project Planning Considerations Framework'. *[see BONUS MATERIALS]*
- Get input from others. The opportunity to gather other people's opinions and observations could lead to a more successful outcome than you could achieve alone. Guiding questions can best accomplish this, for example, "what is missing from this idea?" or "how can you make it more effective?" enabling you to shape and create interest in the idea among those stakeholders.
- Keep those who contributed in the loop as you progress the idea to launch; this way, they will feel part of the initial idea and be eager to see it succeed.
- Take note of stakeholder input and inform their boss and other key stakeholders of their contribution.

## Piloting ideas for stakeholder buy-in

Piloting ideas are also very effective in professional services firms because they're impermanent and non-threatening. At the same time, Marketing teams proposing complete overhauls of existing go-to-strategies can make it difficult for those who have invested in certain concepts to accept your proposal fully.

1. Define your idea's success by identifying how it directly contributes to the firm's goals.
2. Be sure your idea is supported by senior stakeholders (most of them), and each stakeholder knows what you expect of them.
3. Focus on tactics that allow the data you wish to present to be verifiable, such as a webinar that shows the number of registrants and attendees and crucial information about each person, so you can gauge interest in the topic and develop qualified leads.

4. Present your results and show how they support your more significant thesis.

5. Ask for resources and support to expand your original idea to a broader target audience.

In this way, if the pilot does not work, you have saved time and money by not wasting time and money on unproven initiative. It could be that the webinar example above proved to be ineffective.

---

# Expert view

Ben Kent, Founding Director at Meridian West, based in London:

---

*"Running thought leadership and other marketing initiatives can be one of the most rewarding parts of your role. It is an opportunity to explore the latest issues, collaborate with industry experts and use your creativity to help your firm position itself in the market.*

*But it can also be hard work. How do you find a new angle on a topic that will be relevant for your clients? How do you motivate your partners to talk about business (not just technical) issues? How do you avoid project drift? How do you get stakeholders to support your ideas?*

*Based on two decades of creating over 80 campaigns for professional services firms. The following is best practice for planning and securing buy-in for your ideas.*

*Often professional services firms launch straight into execution without devoting enough time to planning marketing initiatives.*

*First, I would recommend running an "Ideas Lab" to identify and refine thought leadership topics with your stakeholders. Form a workshop lasting around 90-minutes. Face to face is best, but if you need to run it online, it is good to use collaboration tools like Miro or Mural to capture ideas. Invite your firms' subject matter experts, marketing and PR, research, brand, design, and other teams.*

*Recommended Ideas Lab Agenda:*

- *Why - defining your goals*

- *The big Idea - what is the story you want to tell?*

- *Audience - are you targeting the c-suite, the press or specialists?*

- *Business case - Which content will give you the best return on investment?*

- *Inputs - the best research techniques*

- *Outputs- creating digital and hard copy assets*

- *Stakeholder engagement - ensuring your staff and partners use the content with your clients Project planning - critical success factors, budget and timing.*

*Before a campaign can get traction, it is critical to get buy-in from the right people for two key reasons:*

1. *Your thought leadership investment will have a much greater return on investment (ROI) if stakeholders in your firm use it as part of their interactions with clients and prospects. Ensuring you have them on board early helps to set expectations about the level of internal engagement expected.*

2. *Budget holders and decision-makers in your firm are close to clients and their needs. Involving them early on can improve the speed and quality of planning decisions and ensure that outputs are as client-focused as possible.*

*The 'Ideas Lab' will allow you to tackle head-on the challenge of engaging internal audiences from the outset. Whilst involving your peers and key stakeholders will give the marketing initiative structure, direction and a precise measure of outcomes.*

*Without seeking the input of key stakeholders, you might miss key considerations and input. You may have created a fabulous client focus initiative such as a thought leadership report based on cutting edge research, but if your firm's advisors don't use the research to talk to your clients, most of your efforts will be a waste.*

*If thought leadership is new to you, identify your naturally good stakeholders at sales and business development and get them on your side early. They can be advocates for the benefit of thought leadership to others. Also, work closely with your account management teams, and they can often be a more effective channel for sharing insight with clients than partners.*

*Focusing on the conversations and outcomes you want should not be an afterthought but integrated with generating ideas."*

## Driven by solutions

Do you sometimes think of an excellent idea, but then someone finds several problems with it before the details are clearly defined? In the previous section, we discussed the importance of gaining input from your stakeholders and colleagues. How many times have you been overly critical when someone internally asks for help, and you simply say, *"that won't work?"* Then you begin to list the reasons why it won't work!

The irony is that professional service firms provide solutions to their external clients. Yet, they are also problem-driven and risk-averse organisations that instil this culture within themselves.

Your progress will increase if you can participate in solving your colleagues' problems. Leaders have to be willing to take on responsibilities beyond their domain as they advance in their careers.

So, when your colleagues pitch an idea, try keeping an open mind and if anything needs to be changed, do it constructively. You should provide feedback in this way by using a softening statement, such as:

> *"Tom, I'd like to help you develop this idea further by offering some of my initial thoughts, which are X, Y, and Z".*

It is even better to provide examples to validate your feedback using data to demonstrate where this approach has worked for you previously, thus adding credibility to your response. Data-driven marketing and decision making allow you to make decisions based on facts rather than opinions.

## Team process for generating solutions

1. Put a team together to support a colleague or the stakeholder with a problem they're trying to solve.
2. Identifying and defining the actual problem is often the most challenging part of the process, as there can be several underlying issues to resolve. Consider grading them according to their overall impact on the business.
3. As a next step, you will generate possible solutions. Don't worry about the quality at this stage, and it is essential that everyone who participates suggests something. At this stage, don't discuss whether or not ideas will work since this will stifle creativity.
4. Discuss the pros and cons of each of the possible solutions you have come up with together.
5. Choosing the most suitable solution (e.g., it can be delivered within the time, resources, and budget available to you) is now the next step.
6. Plan out what needs to be done and by when. Consider possible blockers and identify the cost of delays that may occur, as discussed previously.
7. Examine progress and performance to determine whether they have led to a solution or advancement. Conduct data analysis and receive feedback from stakeholders to assess and improve similar ideas in the future.

## Expert view

Carolyn Manning, Chief Marketing & BD Officer at Mintz, based in Boston:

*"It is important to be an idea generator and solution-oriented in this profession. Ideas evolve things, and any marketing program - or marketing professional - standing still means your firm quickly becomes obsolete. Sometimes the best new idea is to re-package an old idea that worked (think Coca-Cola Classic, when the company reintroduced the original Coke formula). For example, I know of one large firm that changes the look of their internal communication every six months, so the content looks "new", and advisors retake notice. Many initiatives have a shelf life; revisiting and refreshing tried and tested things can be very effective.*

*I recall hearing a legal industry consultant describe lawyers as negative thinkers by necessity. Clients pay them to identify problems and point out obstacles. It is our job to influence stakeholders and advance new ideas. Be prepared to state your case. Advisors like facts. I've always found it helpful to use specific examples of success (e.g. "this approach worked for so-and-so and here's what they did" or "I heard from my friend at X firm that they have done this with success."). My best ideas have evolved from talking to my peer network at other professional service firms. Knowing how something worked - or failed - at another firm is incredibly helpful, especially when pitching new ideas to teammates. We can all learn from each other in this industry.*

*Make it a personal goal to generate new ideas and solutions and regularly focus on this. Doing this with purpose will help advance your career. Go for a walk and just think, better yet, invite a colleague to join you and walk and talk about a problem you are trying to solve. Idea generation takes time, and you will be well-served if you make time regularly to think about this."*

## Listening intently

Listening to hear stakeholders and colleagues is key to effectively communicating to generate ideas that address stakeholders' needs.

Frequently your attention is split between Teams calls, Whatsapp, and email during meetings, which can mean we don't fully listen, acknowledge the conversation, e.g. *"yes, sure, got it"* or *"what about X?"*.

Instead of responding straight away, you should try to listen carefully and paraphrase what you hear. Ask questions until you sense that there is a mutual understanding. Listen for possible obstacles and opportunities that you may have missed if you jumped into the solution too soon.

## 12

# Managing people and leadership

*"Managers do things right. Leaders do the right thing"*
—*Warren G. Bennis*

## Preparing yourself for management

It is challenging for marketing professionals in the industry to move into roles where they will have to manage other individuals or move to a more senior position in another firm, where they may be required to exhibit leadership and management skills without prior experience of managing others. To prepare for management positions in the future, how do you gather such experience?

Leadership is often associated with managing others, and it is not intrinsic to the concept of leadership that you must supervise people to be a manager. Part of the problem is the word leadership, which confirms our perception of "people leadership", but leadership is about influence and how you can influence people, without the formal title and having to approve their holiday requests.

Being highly visible, results-oriented, and responsible are the keys to developing your influence in the Marketing team. It is crucial to demonstrate these behaviours consistently to build and establish your informal power internally. Expert power can go beyond someone's actual expertise. Even though it takes time to gain power, there are several ways you can gain experience before you have a managerial position.

## Developing manager experience before you become one

- **Transferable skills** - there are many ways to assist, such as coaching, presenting to key stakeholders, recruiting, and leading marketing initiatives. These help you develop the skills needed to oversee and manage others - any of these activities in your career.
- **Seek out experience** - now it's more important than ever for you to identify and emphasise these skills in your CV and at your following interview. You should seek such experiences, whether attending recruitment interviews, leading marketing initiatives or mentoring new team members.
- **Upskill gaps** - if you lack the necessary transferable experience, you should take a management course to gain such knowledge quickly. Having a solid background in this field will enhance your career prospects when applying for management roles.
- **Delegate and outsource** - become comfortable delegating or outsourcing specific tasks to specialist teams within your organisation, allowing you to develop people management skills and bring stakeholders together to accomplish objectives.

## Stepping up into management

> *"Listen to all, plucking a feather from every passing goose,*
> *but follow no one absolutely"*
>
> —CHINESE PROVERB

Entering into management for the first time can be problematic, but it's a necessary step to take if you want to grow to be a great leader. At the same time, it is an exciting time in your career, as it means you have mastered a certain level of work and are ready to advance your career forward to take on a new challenge.

The global market has become highly competitive and candidate short, which requires Marketing departments and line managers to focus on talent development and retention. To ensure you keep your most talented individuals and ensure your team continues to create real value for your firm, your approach to management needs to create a workplace in which your team is:

1. treated with respect
2. set clear expectations of their role and how their efforts aligns with the firm's strategy
3. opportunities to use their skills and abilities at work.
4. trusted with crucial information and challenging initiatives
5. protected and supported when working with difficult stakeholders or when conflicts arise
6. learning and continuous improvement culture

### In practice

I have had several line managers and mentors over the course of my career. Each of them is unique in their leadership approach and their specific behaviour when managing me and helping me develop in my career.

Each possesses different strengths and weaknesses. When I stepped into my first manager role, I vowed to take the best behaviours and leadership attributes these individuals displayed and imitate them in my approach to managing others.

The key to succeeding in a management role is to reflect on your career journey and identify which individual leadership styles have you seen as most effective and in line with your values and personality, which you can incorporate into your leadership style.

## Succeeding in a Management role

Whether you are managing a small team at the supervisor level, which is often the case in lean Marketing teams, or are making the step up to a director or CMO role where you are responsible for leading a big department at your firm, your main concerns are likely to be the same;

- How will I know if my leadership is working?
- How do I set effective goals for my team to keep them performing at the highest levels?
- What will my position as a team leader mean? Does this mean I can't be 'one of the team' anymore?
- How will I motivate everyone every day?
- What if the team doesn't like me as their manager? What will I do?
- How do I retain my best talent? Train staff for the marketing skills needed by the firm?
- Where do I have gaps in specialisms?

## Becoming a leader in a changing world

Thanks to advances in technology, sophisticated data-gathering, and new perspectives, marketing professionals' roles within firms have evolved significantly. CMOs are among the most prominent examples of these changes. The skills required in this high-level leadership position are broad and diverse.

First and foremost, CMOs are managers. They hold this position because they also possess leadership and coaching skills on top of technical marketing skills.

Traditionally, CMOs have needed leadership skills, but the future CMO needs to adapt to younger generations' changing interests and work habits. It is common for CMOs to have a management team that consists of older millennials and leading others who are entry-level professionals fresh out of university. The millennial generation is digitally minded, meaning they expect and are dependent on technology to be creative, communicate and work smartly.

Team structures are evolving in Marketing departments in firms, and teams are more specialist and have adopted hybrid working around the globe. Thus, becoming a CMO depends significantly on the versatility to interact with and lead various dedicated teams. Keeping everyone unified on the same cohesive strategy is crucial.

**Expert view**  Zelinda Bennett, Chief Marketing Officer at DWF, based in Manchester:

*"When it comes to leadership, you should start by trying to understand what makes you tick and what type of leader you are. The more you know about yourself - your natural behavioural style, strengths and weaknesses - the better equipped you will be to lead. I'm a big fan of using the following self-assessment tools Myers Briggs and DiSC.*

*In my role as a CMO, where I am responsible for leading a global team, the following has always guided me throughout my career when it comes to people management and leadership in the sector.*

- *You are only as good as your team so ensure you have a strong senior team by surrounding yourself with a diverse group of better people than you. Understand their areas of expertise, their working styles and invest time in them.*

- *A geographically disparate team needs transparency; they want to understand the business's strategy and regularly communicate. I run a series of regular meetings that cover crucial projects and activities.*

- *If the team understands the firm's strategy, it is easier to positively set objectives and performance management. Every day is a performance review! Don't wait for annual performance reviews.*

- *It's also important to be accessible, so any team member needs to know they can contact me any time. Don't forget to say thank you and give praise for a job well done - basics I know but often forgotten.*

- *Be authentic, but that doesn't mean you can misbehave! Think about how people experience you - how do they feel after a meeting/ call with you?*

- *Invest in your team – be prepared to walk in their shoes – are you aware of the daily challenges they face?*

- *Listen to your team – great ideas, best practice and innovation could come from anyone! Make the most of employee engagement surveys and ask your team for feedback.*

- *As a leader, you will need to make some tough decisions. Be brave, make them and be prepared to tackle the fallout – you will learn from any mistakes.*

- *It's okay to fail – if you're not failing, you're not learning – fail fast.*

- *Culture is everything. Ensure that you understand the culture and time zones for those you work with within the team. I highly recommend "When Cultures Collide" by Richard D Lewis."*

---

### ➡ Key points to remember

1. To be a leader, you don't have to supervise people. It's about influence and how you can influence people.

2. To succeed in a management role, you must reflect on your career journey and identify which individual leadership styles, which align with your values and personality, you can incorporate into your leadership style.

3. As a leader, you are only as good as your team, so surround yourself with a diverse group of people who are better than you. Take the time to learn about their areas of expertise and working styles.

4. Develop skills in people management by delegating and outsourcing sp tasks within your company to expert teams, allowing you to bring stakeholders together and achieve objectives.

# PART FOUR

# Internal stakeholder management

*"To keep everyone invested in your vision, you have to back up a little bit and really analyze who the different stakeholders are and what they individually respond to"*
*—Alan Stern*

A marketer's primary responsibility is to engage with external clients strategically. However, the real challenge of delivering products and services to your clients depends on your ability to manage and influence your internal stakeholders.

Your firm consists of diverse teams and functions. That can lead to roadblocks in achieving your objectives and meeting senior stakeholders' needs crucial to your promotional prospects because each department has different objectives and personalities.

You will often find yourself in a situation where you have to convince someone to do something they don't want to do or attempt to change a stakeholder's opinion. In the professional services sector, you will often have no authority over peers and senior stakeholders. Therefore it will be vital to deploy upward influence to influence those in a higher position to follow your lead.

To progress into a senior role, you must have good internal stakeholder management skills and influence others to reach your personal goals.

# 13

# Developing your internal brand

*"Your brand is what other people say about you when you're not in the room"*
*—Jeff Bezos*

## Reinforcing your brand

If no one sees how you are directly contributing to the firm's strategy and no one is championing you in your firm, your stakeholders will overlook you, therefore you will not be in consideration for career opportunities within your firm.

By enhancing your brand, you can distinguish yourself from your peers and position yourself for promotion. To establish and reinforce your career image, you must build and manage your reputation. Positively influencing your internal reputation will improve your chances of promotion, salary increases, create opportunities to work on more exciting initiatives and be involved more in essential decisions in your firm.

To accomplish this, you should be recognised internally as proactive and seek out the most challenging work opportunities that will allow you to gain the knowledge and reputation as someone who can contribute to similar work of this type in the future. The key to this is to consider where you want to be in a few years and think which specific activities will help you build the personal brand you need to reach this objective.

If you are in the early stages of your career, you are likely to attend meetings internally and only focus on listening. If you are not actively contributing to the discussion in meetings, you will likely go unnoticed. To effectively participate in the debate, you need to ask at least one question or provide your input on something that will add meaningful value. To do this effectively, you need to prepare beforehand. Actively contributing will thus raise your profile among other stakeholders who attend, which could mean they invite you to give your input during future meetings.

A key aspect of developing your internal brand at your firm is networking and building relationships internally. It requires you to actively raise your visibility and engage with people outside your immediate team. Learn more about others you meet in training courses or passing, and look for ways you might be able to help one another based on your specialisation or connect them with your internal contacts who are working towards a similar goal. It is a good idea to attend company events, team lunches, and coffee with coworkers. Your colleagues will speak highly of you if you develop close relationships with them, and opportunities will come your way.

## Expert view

Rachel Kennedy, European Law Firm Business Development Manager at Ropes & Gray LLP, based in London:

*"It takes hard work and time to develop your internal brand and reputation. You need to be consistent with your approach and be patient with your stakeholders, but once they trust you, you will be on a fast track to develop your career and receive the best opportunities. Some practical guidance on what has worked for me in my career is to:*

*Don't forget the basics; it may sound simple, but doing the basic tasks correctly, on time, and as requested will show trustworthiness and com-*

petence. There is nothing more frustrating to a senior stakeholder than repeating instructions or correcting basic mistakes that could've been caught with a five-minute proofread.

Communication is vital; ensure you acknowledge emails/requests from stakeholders when they come in. Informing them, you will act on it, even if you can't do it straight away, making them feel important and acknowledged. Also, if you can't deliver when you said you would, as we all know some days don't go as planned, make sure you communicate this to your stakeholders. A senior stakeholder does not need to add chasing to their workload! Also, try to understand the senior stakeholder's preferred communication style is, do they prefer meetings, phone calls, or emails? Once you find this out, you will work more efficiently and effectively with them and not push them out of their comfort zone.

Learn from your mistakes and adopt a growth mindset. Everyone makes mistakes, and that's fine, but not learning from your mistakes and constantly making the same mistake over again can be tiring for senior stakeholders. Learn from your mistakes and adopt a growth mindset. Go on training courses, ask people for advice, develop those skills you don't have or areas less knowledgeable about. Helping you become a well-rounded professional, you are investing in yourself to benefit the business.

Listen carefully and read between the lines, as senior stakeholders are under tremendous pressure, and their time is precious. Regarding work projects, listen carefully to instructions and try to clarify any points you don't understand at the same time. If done over email, think through the whole exercise and go back with any questions in one go. Think of all of the different places you might get the information you need to complete a task first! Drip feeding clarifying questions can be painful for a senior stakeholder. On a personal level, some people are chatty and give lots away in one go, and you can become close quickly; some are more guarded, and it takes longer to build a rapport. You need to listen and analyse what you hear. Once you start listening to what is said, or indeed not said, you will get to know the person much quicker and understand them.

Understand the position of your senior stakeholder and make their life easier. Your senior stakeholder will be under pressure from lots of different *directions. Spend 5 or 10 minutes imagining you are the senior stakeholder and consider their position in the business – who reports to them, whom they report to, their clients, what types of pressure they are under, are they up for promotion, etc. If you can understand their position, you can figure out the best way to help them and make their lives easier.*

*Be positive, as positive things happen to positive people, and your stakeholders will be more willing to seek your expertise out and work with you on this basis."*

## Going beyond "support"

Marketing professionals in the industry are often described as "support" by their firms and stakeholders, compared to advisors who are termed "fee earners." You may encounter internal stakeholders asking you to "jazz" up a document or another task that is not best suited to your expertise.

There is a cultural problem in the industry. Would you ever see B2C companies refer to their marketing and sales functions as "support" functions? Not likely. Marketing drives revenue and enables a business to compete in the market, and neither would function adequately without a unified approach.

You must recognise your value to move beyond "support" at your firm. Like your advisors, you have the relevant education, experience, and insight into planning, developing, and going to market in a relevant field.

Consider your role as someone who should challenge and consult with advisors instead of passively accepting requests to be considered a trusted advisor. Discover their goals, e.g. *"what does success look like?"* or *"why is this important to the company?"* gently challenge their ideas through a validated learning experience. Also, don't hesitate to offer your recommendations; remember that you are an expert on the topic, so you are well-positioned to advise what partners can do to succeed.

---

**Expert view**   Rhys Calcott, Co-Head, Global Client Development
at Slaughter and May, based in London:

---

*"Being perceived in the right way by key stakeholders is crucial to achieving success and going beyond being considered "support" to be considered a trusted advisor to your stakeholders. You must think about it carefully and prioritise it as a tool for making things happen. You may have all the best ideas in the world, but without decision-makers buy-in, you won't move the needle and achieve positive outcomes. The following tips are behaviours I have personally followed throughout my career and stand by now I'm in a management position:*

*Deference to partners is an easy trap to fall into given their status, experience and knowledge, but our role is to advise and challenge. To do that effectively, you need to converse on an even-par basis. Being overly submissive and 'giving in' will damage your brand. That said, know when to push and when to back away.*

*Always be authentic and approach things to suit your style and feel natural. Not to say that you shouldn't push yourself to achieve more and stretch, but don't attempt to imitate others.*

*You are a specialist in what you do. Partners are experts at law, accounting or other consulting services. Still, we must demonstrate our knowledge and strategic ability in our natural area of specialism to build trust, respect and achieve buy-in.*

*Exude confidence in everything you do. People buy from those they believe in and trust. You must show confidence in your approach for others to follow.*

*When prepping for meetings/presentations, always anticipate the questions and challenges you'll receive. You'll be well prepared to respond swiftly and confidently to win over your audience. It also helps you plan what your successful outcome will be.*

*If you have ambitions to progress and climb, learn from those twice above you. I've always observed how my boss's boss operates, seeing that role as my stretch and longer-term goal.*

*Live and work with the stop, think, challenge and deliver mantra. Never accept a request or idea at face value. Pause and consider, ask the right questions, and understand what we are trying to achieve and the best possible outcome for our clients. Then challenge/persuade/advise, thus moving you away from being viewed as a "doer" and someone who reacts to someone who is an adviser. Once you've convinced them of your proposal - you must deliver. Hit all four steps every time, and you will build that trusted adviser status."*

## Introducing yourself: crafting the perfect elevator speech

For larger firms, you will have to introduce yourself regularly. Thus, practising your elevator pitch is crucial, so you didn't simply mumble your job title when next asked to introduce yourself. Getting this right is essential, as you want stakeholders to be curious and engaged about what you have to say and how you can help them.

Think about why stakeholders will benefit from working with you, such as:

> *"In my role as a Marketing Executive, I am responsible for growing our firm's brand as well as taking on new clients in Y".*

Then, back your claim up with evidence of past success (using data).

You can now develop your elevator pitch based on the above method. Believe in it, get comfortable saying it. Next time someone asks you to introduce yourself, make it count!

## Become indispensable

What is the best way to transition from being viewed as merely an "adviser" or supporter for stakeholders' marketing whims into someone who can help guide the strategy, serve as an advisor, and add real value?

To become indispensable, one must be reliable to stakeholders and knowledgeable in areas in demand.

1. **Reliability** - be regarded by stakeholders as someone they can rely on for urgent and complex initiatives. It's essential to show up and follow through on your commitments.

2. **Expert** - as well as being reliable, you must become the go-to person for your area, monopolising the knowledge or skill you possess. Therefore, you will become indispensable when stakeholders require specific help with a task you know well.

It is a gradual process built on hard work, proactiveness, and ultimately, trust.

## Establishing expert power

In your firm, you will often be working with senior stakeholders and peers over whom you have no authority, so it is challenging for you to influence them into changing their behaviour and attitude.

Deep, underlying power comes from discovering and solving other stakeholders' needs. Everyone has pain or a problem they want or need solving, but you may have to dig deep. By establishing yourself as an expert because of the skills, knowledge and expertise, you possess will give you the power to influence the decisions of your peers and seniors, as they will respect your opinion on certain matters more.

To do this you must grow and develop your expertise from informational sources. [see CHAPTER 17]

---

### In practice

Before joining Eversheds Sutherland as sector group manager for the industrial sector, I had no experience working in a sector role. I did not know much about aerospace, automotive, or chemicals.

---

To understand clients and provide practical advice to internal stakeholders regarding our firm's positioning within these sectors, I needed to develop a comprehensive knowledge of these sectors.

To prepare for this, I read as many white papers as possible, spent my time working out whilst listening to podcasts about the aerospace industry; I learned more about the sector than my stakeholders. I would post daily sector news items on LinkedIn and regularly share sector news with internal stakeholders. As my understanding developed, I would go one step further and add my options and commentary when sharing on LinkedIn.

Through these activities, I quickly established myself as a valuable individual to my stakeholders in understanding the sector and the clients that operate within it.

## Process of building trust with internal stakeholders

You have to recognise that each of your internal stakeholders are made up of different groups and individuals with their own unique differences, what works for one individual might not work as well for others.

Thus, gradually building your relationships with the below steps is imperative. Specific stakeholders will make it easier to move forward quickly, while others will struggle to recognise your value past the stage of "trust".

1. **Awareness** - there will be an issue that needs to be solved by an internal stakeholder. They will have been directed to you by a colleague or your boss for you to handle. They have never heard of you or worked with you, so they will be unsure of your knowledge and skills. Scoping precisely what is required and assisting them in resolving their problems efficiently and effectively will help you create positive first impressions. Additionally, you can use this stage to build awareness with a broader group of stakeholders in the business that probably hasn't heard about you yet, enabling you to build advocates who will champion your work within the firm.

2. **Understanding** - once they understand your role, they will know how you can help them in the future. Still, the stakeholder spends time with you going over the details and scoping out precisely what is needed. They're likely to check in regularly on the progress since they'll be unfamiliar with how quickly you can complete the task.

3. **Acceptance** - you have now reached the point where they accept your skills and knowledge as valuable to them. You have likely continued to do an excellent job on the initiatives and requests they have worked with you on. Based on your previous performance, they avoid spending as much time on the details and assume you know what they want to do, so make sure you scope it correctly.

4. **Trust** - at this point, you have developed a strong level of trust. Your someone trusted now to fulfil the request. No longer will you be micromanaged.

5. **Strategic advisor** - The relationship will decrease informality as you develop a bond as a strategic advisor. After working with you first hand, they will be more inclined to listen to your advice, since they trust your expertise and reputation. They will seek opportunities to praise you in front of your boss and other senior stakeholders.

---

**Expert view**     Daniel Tompsett, Elvis Yarda, and Alistair Brisbourne, Research & Commercial Insights gurus for a top Accounting and Advisory firm, the team based in London:

---

*"As a research offering within a leading Accountancy and Advisory firm, we reached a crossroads with how we were dealing with our internal stakeholders. We wanted to grow our commercial insights offering alongside supporting partners' broader marketing-led research requirements. However, given the level of day-to-day demand and the team's small size, we realised we would have to change the way we*

worked to achieve that fundamentally. Here's how we achieved a quiet revolution in the way we interacted with our stakeholders:

There is always a certain percentage of what we do that we enjoy less than everything else in every role. Left unchecked, you may even feel as if you are only doing stuff you hate doing. It can happen because we allow stakeholders to lead us in what we do 100% of the time. If we enable stakeholders to direct what we are doing and when we are doing it, stakeholders can quash a piece of our creative humanity. Secondly, our stakeholders won't respect us because they only view us as a "resource". Worker bees for stakeholders get one thing above all else in their career – more work. But they have no input on what they are doing, how to go about it or why they are doing it. To change that, you have to find a way to strictly not do stuff you hate. As part of our research team, we took brave steps in that direction in the following ways:

Learn to say "no": saying no is hard. That is until you do it. If you can do it once, you realise you could do it again and then again and again. In the end, you will become a sceptic. You will be sceptical about each request asked of you. Also, therefore, increasing the quality of thinking going in and seeking an understanding from the stakeholder, whether you can do it. It is also suitable for you because it means you will do less stuff you hate. There is a balance, of course, and no; you cannot say "no" to everything, but everything should be subject to rigorous scrutiny as to why you are doing it. Carry out thoughtful and engaging discussions with stakeholders;

Learn to put a value on it: to stop doing stuff you hate, it is also essential to have a keen sense of the importance of what you are being asked to do. The quickest way to do that is to ask the ROI question. Ask your stakeholder what the ROI would be for the firm if you undertook that task. Your time has value. The value is what the firm pays you, let's say, by the hour. If someone is asking to extract four hours of your time, you know what your salary is worth to the firm. Does what you are doing relate to your priorities, represent an appropriate ROI on that value for the firm? Suppose you cost the firm X to do that work, and the potential value recouped for the firm is only Y. In that case, it is much easier to talk stakeholders out of wasting the firm's precious resources and making themselves less competitive in the market. Thinking in a business-like way is good. Many firms record the *billable time that fee earners accrue in working for clients. It's a good idea to see if You and your team could implement a similar structure.*

*Learn to put up the hand: However, many of the things we hate to land on our desks because we become "yes" people. We are keen to do well and eager to be seen as someone who can deliver solutions and solve any problem. That is fatal. That is route one to becoming a worker bee only for our stakeholders, and we know worker bees only get one thing. Rather than saying "yes" to the next job requesting your input on your desk, before running through the potential of applying the steps outlined above, always put up your hand. By putting up the hand, we mean "stop". When someone is rambling to you about why they need ten thousand lines of data or a pitch with a picture of a digger on the front, always, always hold up your hand. Next, ask them for a clear written brief. What is it they are looking to do? Such is the power of the hand. It will ensure that they have to sit down and think through what they are asking of you to document it before you even get the request. Never, ever commit to doing the job on the spot.*

*The power of the hand is such that you can leave the request zone, saying, "send me a detailed brief, and I will assess it and let you know the best way we can get that done." That way, you have achieved three things. Firstly, you have made them a stakeholder with you in what they ask you to do. Focus on stakeholders' minds and precisely the actual value of what they ask. If they can't be bothered to think through and write a short but detailed brief, then why should you bother to do the work! Secondly, you have ensured that you get a push back opportunity to be part of the thinking of the "why?" of this task when their written brief lands or just in a deeper discussion. Thirdly, you have built-in time. Time means proper thought all around. The adequate idea means measuring ROI and time value, and then and only then can you give the stakeholder the correct answer for the firm's profitability, which might be "yes", but it also might be "no". Remember, this is a business, and you are one of the gatekeepers in the business as to what constitutes good business sense;*

*If you are successful in the above strategies for not doing stuff you hate, then the first thing you will earn yourself is time. Time is a very precious commodity, and you know what it is worth to you and the firm because you know what your salary is, and hopefully, you now know what your time value on a job is. The second thing you will have done is transform the perception of you in the eyes of your stakeholder from worker bee to the coveted role of an Advisor. Worker bees are arguably more difficult to promote because they are overcapacity, under a great wall of work that might fall if moved.*

*The next phase involves putting on the Advisor roles and going out and proactively advising people on what the firm should do next. You have accrued time, but now it is time to reinvest that time for the firm's benefit and work. Suddenly, your stakeholders ask you for answers as to what direction they should be working in to achieve success. Suddenly they look less like stakeholders in what you deliver to them, and they start to look like they are stakeholders in your ideas and following your lead. We did it as a team and ushered in a quiet revolution successfully. There is no doubt that you could do it too."*

## Staying visible

The outbreak of the COVID-19 will have forced you to work from home and change your working style. Resulting in you clocking extra hours, going to additional meetings for face time with specific individuals, and spending more time with line managers so they can see your efforts and the hours you log.

Maintaining relevance requires you to be proactive. In the same way, your firm engages with its clients, assesses how you can add value, such as sharing knowledge or up-to-date news about a client.

As your firm adapts to new ways of working, whether you are now working on a hybrid basis or fully remote, staying visible will become more critical than ever for your career advancement. You will have limited facetime with your boss and key stakeholders, if not implemented.

To maintain positive relationships and an effective work environment, it is essential to make your presence known more than ever.

## Strategies for maintaining visibility when working remotely

1. **Continued progress** - Ensure you keep your work moving and provide regular status updates; this way, your line manager and stakeholders can see you are on top of your workload. Daily or weekly emails, adding to your schedule of talking points to discuss with your manager.

2. **Create consistent and regular touchpoints** - make an effort each week to connect with a few colleagues outside your direct team or key stakeholders. It can be as simple as checking in on how they are doing, how you can support them, or sending them helpful information.

3. **Speak up and show up** - there is increased importance on the level of input you provide during meetings when working remotely. To help you improve your visibility, ensure you turn your camera on and contribute to each discussion.

4. **Become a team player** - in firms where you have colleagues scattered across the continent or globe, partaking in various firmwide charity initiatives and other related activities. It is a great way to remind people of who you are and your extracurricular interests. Using LinkedIn is an excellent way to communicate this through posting on your LinkedIn page for your colleagues and others at your company to see, and this allows them to engage with you.

### In practice

When I began working in a global firm of Eversheds Sutherland's size, I found it difficult to interact with multiple stakeholders worldwide. To develop my internal network around the globe and increase visibility, I utilised LinkedIn to connect and stay connected with my stakeholders.

I connected with all the key stakeholders I worked with actively and other senior stakeholders across the business that I wanted to develop a relationship with. Later on, we will cover the importance of clearly identifying the VIP stakeholders that you want to engage with regularly. At first, I felt uncomfortable doing this but convinced myself that this was the best approach for these busy stakeholders to know who I was. As soon as we connected on LinkedIn, I regularly did the following:

- Post firm updates on my social media feed, so they would appear in their newsfeed.

- Engage with their posts by liking and commenting on them (making sure to tag them, so they receive a notification using "@[their name]").

- Share relevant industry information, if you have a sector-specific position.

As the world becomes increasingly virtual, it will be harder for you to remain visible to your peers and senior stakeholders, so implementing the above is essential.

 **Key points to remember**

1. Recognise yourself as an expert and someone that can add meaningful value to the work you are involved with your internal stakeholders

2. Create and practice your elevator speech to introduce yourself internally and externally

3. Become reliable and knowledgeable in areas in demand to become indispensable

4. Maintaining your global network and visibility through LinkedIn is an excellent way to connect and stay visible with your key internal stakeholders.

# 14

# Influencing others and avoiding conflicts

*"The greatest ability in business is to get along with others and influence their actions"*
*—John Hancock*

## Keeping others motivated

Firms consist of highly educated, time-pressed, and relatively autonomous professionals that need to be persuaded and be motivated to work together in a highly competitive environment to serve their clients. Individuals in an organisation have different objectives and receive remuneration differently, making this particularly challenging when your marketing initiatives success relies on motivating them.

When delivering marketing initiatives, advisors play an irreplaceable role as they possess the technical knowledge you likely do not have. Therefore you will often find yourself in a situation whereby you will be required to upwardly influence someone to do something or convince them to contribute to a marketing initiative you are working on for you to achieve your objectives.

To ask advisers to help you on a project, you must influence them to help you in the right way. Avoid the typical approach many do in the Marketing team, where they ask partners, *"can you write an article on Y?"* or *"can we talk about Y at our conference?"*. The demands of internal and external stakeholders need consideration. The problem with this approach is that you are trying to influence senior stakeholders over who you have no authority over which often results in them resisting.

Instead, you should look to "sell" them the benefits of being involved by explaining how this will benefit them; this type of tactic will often result in them being more compliant and hopefully committed to your initiative. Finding ways to motivate others requires understanding how they are motivated and encouraging them. Before asking or communicating with stakeholders, ask yourself, "what's in it for me?" (WIIFM). You have to assume that to influence others; you need to identify and then convey how the other person will benefit/gain by doing what you ask.

For example, when you are asking them for input into your next client briefing, you might frame how you motivate others as follows:

> *"Would you be interested in providing content for our next client briefing that we will send to 8,000+ of our closest contacts around the world?"*

Rather than asking them to give up their time to present at the next client conference, you might approach them as follows:

> *"We are hosting our key client conference, which we can expect to have over 100+ clients in attendance if you were to speak on topic Y. We believe clients would consider us for work in this area."*

An alternative way to gain buy-in and advocacy for your idea is to seek out and create "idea champions", who will share your vision of its tangible and intangible benefits to the firm after learning about your idea.

The key to developing an idea champion is to connect with the person emotionally. They need to see the benefits of supporting your idea, which could be helping them win new clients or providing better service to existing clients. These champions will help motivate others and act as catalysts for its implementation.

To add further social proof to your ideas, seek out those stakeholders within the firm that possess influence and authority, as this will lead to others following their lead if they trust and back your idea.

## Expert view
Koree Khongphand-Buckman, Chief Marketing and Business Development Officer at Foley & Lardner, based in Denver:

*"Logic tells us that you are much more likely to succeed in your initiatives if you have the unyielding support of the majority of all stakeholders involved in delivering an industry. However, influencing stakeholders in the professional services sector can often be challenging regardless of your title or influence within the firm. Throughout my career in the industry, I have found success in winning partners over and securing their buy-in in a few different ways:*

*The first is to spend time getting to know them. It sounds simple, but investing in relationships and building rapport with the partners in your firm can go a long way toward establishing trust and gaining their confidence (which ultimately can give you more power to affect change).*

*The second way is to show how your vision and goals align with the firm's strategic plan. In short, this underscores that you know what you're doing - you understand the firm's overall priorities, and your initiatives will contribute to helping achieve them.*

*The third way is to demonstrate that you understand their practice, clients, and pain points. Whenever possible, please provide examples of how you're capable of assisting your partners with their professional goals. If they understand where you can provide value, they are more likely to support your ideas.*

*Lastly, and perhaps most importantly, do the little things well and deliver them on time (if not early). Developing a solid reputation among your partners is mission-critical - they will be much more inclined to allow you to try new, more significant initiatives if you nail the small stuff."*

## Deploying Accountability Traps

Have you ever declined a new request because you were too busy or kept putting it off because it wasn't urgent, but then your boss got involved and asked you to prioritise it?

If you aren't making progress, a viable alternative or last resort is to implement an accountability trap. Since everyone has a boss, if you identify their boss and approach them to encourage them to take on the task, the individual will further become part of the initiative.

For example, say you approach a specific team for your conference as per the above, instead of going to a particular individual, you should email the head of the group. Request they nominate someone you can hold accountable, e.g.

> "We are hosting a key client conference next month, and we think your team has a unique perspective on Y, which clients would be interested in. To position our understanding on this topic firmly in our client's minds, who from your team could I involve as part of this conference?"

If partners see you working with other partners, which results in positive ROI and feedback, they will be more engaged in listening and working with you.

## Resolving disputes

You will inevitably face tensions with stakeholders, regardless of how thoroughly you plan the initiative. Several reasons can contribute to this, including things going wrong, delays occurring, or expectations not being met. The ability to handle disputes as they arise will help you build a strong reputation when these scenarios occur and make sure your key stakeholder relationships are protected.

Miscommunication and acting on assumptions are two of the leading causes of tension. To resolve this issue, follow these steps:

- **Reflect on stakeholder comments** - it is critical to demonstrate that you understand their concerns. In other words - *"Just to clarify, you're unhappy because [insert their reason in your own words]."*
- **Commit** - every person makes mistakes. Accept full responsibility, don't blame others, own the error, and develop an action plan on how to fix it.
- **Improve** - for significant initiatives, if elements were missed or not handled properly in the original scope, make sure you review the lessons learned next time **[see CHAPTER 8]**.

There will be times when miscommunication or a critical stakeholder will go off to someone senior in the Marketing team, and they could include you in this witch hunt.

Determine what may have happened, who may be at fault, and what may be possible in the future. Try to smooth this out if you are in the wrong. Examine emails, notes, and evidence if necessary.

It is crucial to your brand and career prospects within your firm, and you should always strive to protect it and ensure that it never tarnishes. As a result of a diverse group of personalities and many deadlines everyone is working to meet, there will be conflicts.

## Dealing with difficult stakeholders

- Keeping your cool, receiving a complaint or hearing stakeholders' rant is never pleasant, but you must avoid becoming defensive or argumentative.
- When working on a marketing initiative, identify difficult stakeholders and monitor them closely. Additionally, figure out what motivates them specifically.
- When dealing with these stakeholders, you need to be open and understand their perspectives. Understanding their viewpoint is crucial, as people want to feel understood and like their opinions matter.

- Know what motivates them - why do they resist? If you can identify the underlying motivations for their resistance, you can more effectively identify areas for compromise to create win/win scenarios and take a project forward.
- Equip yourself with data and facts to support your point of view.

When you reach senior roles, you will be managing upwards, downwards, and across the firm; therefore, it's inevitable you will come across conflicts, whether this relates to differences of opinion, disputes of responsibility, or interpersonal conflicts. It will be crucial that you develop the skills to deal with conflicts effectively. In a senior position, you will be working closely with senior stakeholders across the firm, so you need to be seen as someone willing to see the bigger picture, consider alternatives, and wants to find the best win-win outcome.

 **Key points to remember**

1. Adopt a collaborative approach when trying to get buy-in from stakeholders

2. Motivate others by identifying their motivation and "selling" them on the benefits

3. Ensure you resolve disputes quickly - reflect, commit, and improve

4. Identify difficult stakeholders and monitor them closely on any of your initiatives they are involved with

# 15

# Managing and organising stakeholders

*"Always deliver more than expected"*
*—Larry Page*

## Internal Client Excellence

Building off of the last chapter, which focused on how you should look to build trust and visibility. Now, we need to focus on how you should look to bring "excellence" to each piece of work you deliver to your internal stakeholders. Focus on treating your internal stakeholders the same way firms handle their meaningful external client relationships:

- **Identify expectations upfront (scoping)** - key to scoping new requests is to ask good questions to clarify what they want to achieve, as this helps you approach the task in the right way. Also, capturing information efficiently, if you get this part wrong and misunderstand what is required, you will have to redo it, which wastes everyone's time. *[Use 'Key Project Plan' TEMPLATE]*

- **Keep them updated with progress** - frequent communication is vital to maintain a good relationship with your internal stakeholders. Agree as part of the scoping process when they expect to receive progress updates from you.

## In practice

Undoubtedly one of the most important habits to form as you take ownership of more initiatives or specific actions. Early on in my career at Slaughter and May, it was customary for me to be handling several tasks from multiple stakeholders. I would often take these on and prioritise when stakeholders demanded each request. At my firm, my manager pointed out that it was critical that I clarify the expectations of my stakeholders for each new request and, more essential, update them throughout the task. Whether preparing research ahead of a client meeting or collating relevant information for pitches, each of these tasks had a deadline. Stakeholders were counting on my input to help them move forward with their duties, whether preparing for the client meeting or delivering the pitch to stakeholders to review before sending it to the client. Communication is fundamental; we all have competing tasks. We're confronted with challenges that might delay when we can deliver on our jobs, and it becomes vital that we manage expectations and keep regularly communicating with stakeholders. The last thing you want is stakeholders chasing for an update.

- **Responsive** - your internal stakeholders are busy and under pressure; often, they need reassurance that their messages are received, prioritised and acted promptly. It should not be unreasonable for them to expect a reply to emails, phone calls and MS Teams within 24 hours. Sometimes you will not respond straight away, so you should send a quick message to confirm you have received it and will review or respond shortly. Think if others did this for the emails you sent, how much less time would you have to chase or get frustrated wondering when someone will ever respond?

- **Follow-up** - a crucial part of your development and continuing to improve (Kaizen), is following up with internal stakeholders to hear from and engage with them around how they thought the initiative went. Using such an opportunity to demonstrate the ROI of the overall initiative and evidence the value your support has made in achieving these results will help you build a stronger relationship in the future.

## Expert view

Laura Ottley, Director of Business Development at Addleshaw Goddard, based in London:

*"Being good at the tactical elements of the job will only take you so far. How you handle relationships with your stakeholders is essential. So how do you build your reputation amongst stakeholders and succeed in your career? For me, make sure you have an excellent communication style.*

*Communicate regularly. It sounds simple, except it doesn't happen anywhere near often. Partners expect quick responses to emails as they want to know if you are on to it. Usually, marketing people wait until they have the complete answer before replying to an email. You are far better at acknowledging the email and saying you will get back to them in the next couple of days with the next steps. Reassuring people that you are on to it and gives them confidence. It is also an excellent opportunity for you to manage when they are likely to receive an answer, which allows you to be realistic with your stakeholders.*

*Often Partners ask for things, and we assume that every request is urgent. But so often, it isn't. If you don't ask, you're likely to rush, possibly panic, make poor decisions and ultimately let yourself and your internal client down. Clarifying the deadline and agreeing on it upfront is a far better way of handling the situation. If you cannot meet the timescale, then be upfront. People respond far better to honesty than saying you will do it, only to miss the deadline then. Taking the time to ask questions about the task is so important. Unpacking the desired outcome and purpose adds value and avoids responding to ill-conceived, half-baked requests and need for sense checking.*

*Good relationship managers have good dialogue, ask what someone is trying to achieve with the task, and clarify the requirements before rushing in. Partners will respect your critical thinking and challenges. If they don't agree with your review or you find yourself struggling, escalate it to your manager. Too often, marketing people struggle alone to handle situations. Your managers are there to support you. They are also there to help you prioritise. Usually, I have found junior colleagues, in particular, are incredibly busy but often busy with tasks that are the least important and take up a disproportionate amount of time. Good stakeholder management knows when to work on suitable projects, planning, understanding competing interests to manage conflicts of interest, and managing communication. Line Managers have an essential role to play here, but whatever level you're operating at, the best advice I can offer is to avoid using too much email. The more you can do on calls and face to face, the better. Challenge yourself to ensure you have regular two-way dialogue a day, not on email.*

*Communication is also about making sure you have a voice. In meetings, speak up. I don't think my idea might be correct, or I am not senior enough to make a point. You are in a meeting for a reason, so be present and active. People respect those that have ideas and can engage others in them.*

*Finally, being a good communicator is essential for having conversations about your career aspirations. Make sure you always ask others for feedback on your performance in projects to learn from it. At appraisal meetings, be honest about your career aspirations with your manager. Don't just wait to be asked if you want a promotion, and ask which areas you need to develop in to move you forward."*

## Capturing information effectively

Taking good notes of any action or critical information is an important habit I was taught early on in my career; capturing this information makes it easier to review it later. When receiving new requests and scoping out what is required of busy stakeholders, clarifying details already discussed previously can cause frustration and waste stakeholders time, which is finite and valuable to your firm.

Whatever your preferred method of capturing information, whether it be a notepad, or notes on the phone, make sure you do it, and you can refer back to it.

You don't need to capture what was spoken word-for-word, but your notes should be helpful to refer back to for crucial information and understanding what your commitments are following a meeting or discussion. Critical information to capture:

- **Action items** - the most critical information to capture as these help everyone move forward. A simple format is - *[Specific request] - (responsible person) if time-sensitive, you can also add a due date, e.g. [by X]*
- **Key notes** - use your best judgement regarding which discussion elements to capture during internal meetings. If your gut is that some may need to be reviewed later, better to note down.
- **Research** - at times, you will not understand all of the information you will capture during meetings and discussions with stakeholders, whether technical or an unfamiliar topic. To ensure you develop your knowledge, make a note of these to research later. This will also help you to understand key points from the meeting.

## VIP Prioritisation

Regarding your career progression at your firm, not all stakeholders are created equal in importance and relevance. How do you identify the right ones, and how do you manage them?

Stakeholder groups are often diverse at larger firms, spanning various departments, locations, and jurisdictions. The most important thing to consider when developing initiatives is who is involved, their level of influence within your organisation, and their seniority level.

Senior partners may not show a high level of interest in specific marketing initiatives. Still, you need their cooperation for projects to launch, e.g. motivating others to engage or certain budgetary items.

Focusing your energy and engagement efforts on vital internal stakeholders will help you advance your career.

If you are applying for a promotion or a job interview [see **CHAPTER 3**], identify potential decision-makers. As often as not, stakeholders outside of marketing will be part of the interview committee, making it imperative that you expand your internal network outside of marketing. Be sure they know who you are, and even better if they have directly worked with you.

Keeping your boss happy is also part of this activity.

## Make Your Boss Look Good

It's not just you who has a boss; everyone does. It is essential to perform consistently and meet the expectations of your boss.

In return, your boss will become your advocate and mentor, opening up a world of opportunities for you.

The way you work and deliver work reflects upon your boss. Perform well, achieve results, and it's a linear process to the top for you both.

Therefore, identifying how you can help your manager succeed in their role is an essential strategy. To achieve this, you must become indispensable to your boss, which you can accomplish in several ways:

- **Become dependable** - increased pressure to exceed stakeholder expectations is more prevalent in senior roles, so your boss will have to turn to you for assistance. Make yourself their go-to person for specific tasks by asking what you can help them with and delivering these services so your manager will come to you for future tasks.

- **Understand their preferences** - learn what they need from you and how they expect you to deliver work and information to them. In many cases, your boss will have to report to his boss and other senior stakeholders, so you must regularly update them and keep them informed. It can be as simple as a weekly update call or email. Once you understand their preferences, you are more likely to gain their trust moving forward.

- **Lighten the load** - by taking specific responsibilities off your manager, and you will make their life easier, allowing them to focus on their responsibilities and particular goals. Having them on your side at work will help you advance your career prospects.

- **Protect them** - make sure your manager is protected, pre-empt and avoid them eer being blindsided. You may have made a significant mistake or upset a substantial stakeholder in the company. Make sure you collect all the relevant information and raise it immediately with your manager. It will ensure you control the message and handle any feedback about your performance. You are also building trust with your manager by being honest and taking responsibility for your mistakes.

- **Know their goals** - ask them often, what are your goals? What can I do to help you achieve this? It is also essential you focus on the right tasks by aligning your priorities.

- **Bring solutions, not problems** - Your manager may have their priorities to complete. As discussed in previous chapters, if you bring solutions, they will view you as a trusted resource for important projects and get your input.

- **Operate self-sufficiently** - as you advance in your career and begin to assume more responsibility, make sure you are proactive in bringing ideas to your boss that will help the company meet its goals. To transition into a senior role, you must anticipate future client needs and not just wait for your manager to direct you and generate all the ideas. As a manager, this is one of the most critical types of behaviour I encourage anyone I work with to develop.

## Presenting your solution to senior stakeholders

When you find yourself tasked with presenting your proposal or idea to senior stakeholders, how will you make it a success? You will engage with them or get the approval necessary to get you started.

Before you load up PowerPoint and spend time thinking about how your presentation will look, think about why your idea will be relevant or appealing to your senior stakeholders?

Then form:

- **Challenge** - what are the challenges you are trying to solve? Why should they care? It would be helpful to clarify this current position using data/case studies/ feedback.

- **Define success** - what are you trying to achieve? Don't list too many items. As you share your vision with them, you can help them visualise its real potential, pique their interest in your presentation.

- **Action plan** - now it's time to present your carefully thought-out action plan. This slide will get the most engagement, so be prepared for questions. Pilot the presentation on a colleague before the main presentation. Clearly describe the key steps and, most importantly, what decisions you need them to make, e.g. budget approvals or their role in your idea (input, influencing others, or other actions). Remember, this is the point of your entire presentation.

When using PowerPoint, make it as simple as possible. Stay away from technical jargon and information overload. Ensure you clearly and concisely communicate the key points you want to convey to ensure maximum impact. Depending upon how well you know your key messages, you may even be able to do so without the slide deck altogether.

This approach is not limited to your firm's external clients; when launching something internally, it can be equally effective and easier to implement if you have the support of a subject matter expert who can support your pilot program.

## Developing an international mindset

To work effectively with your international stakeholders and be successful, you need to have an international mindset to operate and collaborate in a multicultural and global environment. This means developing self-awareness, knowledge and a deep understanding of how different cultures approach business and business relationships. Through this, you will foster strong relationships with international stakeholders and communicate effectively and collaborate on marketing initiatives.

You can take several steps to develop an international mindset and understanding. Investing in developing an understanding and curiosity of your stakeholders' cultural values, behaviour and how these differ across different cultures in the workplace.

Discover the business and social etiquette of other countries. Find out about them online, read about them, and speak with others across your firm and the industry.

What stereotypes do you hold to be true? Is it essential to be aware of your unconscious biases and challenge them regularly? Stereotypes are the result of judgemental attitudes and selective perception. Be curious, open, and willing to learn.

In our digital age, where we have so many options for virtual collaboration, it is easier than ever to collaborate with stakeholders from all over the world.

Make sure you stay informed and educated about global developments. Spending a few minutes each morning reading Google News (World section), which is free and will provide you with a quick overview of what's going on in the world, is an excellent place to start.

Regardless of your firm's size and global footprint, the rapidly developing and competitive international business world means that your ability to communicate effectively in the multicultural workplace is critical. As you move up into senior roles, it becomes increasingly important to demonstrate and gain different perspectives from stakeholders.

**Expert view**   Frances Haughey, Senior Marketing and Business Development Manager (TMT Sector at Eversheds Sutherland, based in Leeds:

*"When working in a global business and as part of a worldwide team, a key element of successful stakeholder management is understanding your target audience and adapting how you work to the stakeholders you are working with around the world. Whilst I am based in the UK, the key stakeholders I work with regularly are those found in the Middle East and the US. Some essential tips I have learned along the way to support working with international stakeholders are:*

- *Always consider different time zones when scheduling meetings – try to stick within core business hours as much as possible. For example, when I am trying to accommodate the UK, Middle East and US (both East and West Coast), I only have a tiny window in the day for meetings all parties can attend (2 pm – 3 pm UK time). Chart different time zones when scheduling meetings so everyone is aware.*

- *Be aware of different important holidays in countries, e.g. Thanksgiving in the US, Chinese New Year, Eid al-Fitr, and avoid scheduling deadlines or events during these periods.*

- *Similarly, be aware of different working patterns – for instance, Friday – Saturday is their weekend in the Middle East. As a result, the working week for teams to work together is only four days, not five. Still, Sunday is a good day for Middle East colleagues to catch up on things throughout the week, so on a Friday, I share a summary of outstanding actions from the week, highlighting those that need prioritising. Similarly, many European countries effectively closed down for the month in August.*

- *Use a reasonably formal tone and style (until you have built good relationships to do otherwise!). Many cultures prefer a traditional business communications style, e.g. Germany and Japan.*

- *Be aware of the different management cultures and approaches to hierarchy in other countries. Always know what you are working and meeting with – note their job titles and roles.*

- *Ways of working – when I first started working with my key stakeholders in the Middle East, I was amazed when they wanted to communicate via WhatsApp; however, this is very common in the Middle East when doing business. Similarly, many people connect with clients and colleagues via social media apps in the US. In contrast, we tend to be more formal in the UK and stick to LinkedIn for work relationships!*

- *Manage expectations and be realistic when setting deadlines. Issuing something on a Thursday for a turnaround on Friday will not work for your stakeholders in the Middle East. Similarly, sending a barrage of emails throughout the UK's working day for colleagues to wake up to in Asia and the US is not always the most excellent way to start your day! Similarly, with any communication, always ask the "so what?" question – why is it relevant/important to that person, what will they take away from it.*

- *Things can get lost in translation – follow up in writing to confirm tasks / what was agreed, in some countries "prioritising" something can mean acting immediately in others – it means they will think about it next week!*

- *Learn about the geopolitical landscapes of the key regions in which you are working and how they impact your business and colleagues*

- *Finally, remember relationships are between people, get to know your colleagues!"*

When you are working on international marketing initiatives, it is essential that you also consider and adapt your marketing planning to assess:

- Is the initiative suitable or applicable in other jurisdictions? Does it need adapting if not?
- Do you have local stakeholders supporting the initiative? have you taken the time to brief the local stakeholders before the initiative is about to launch?
- Have you considered the local time zones and how this will affect deadlines/response speed?

**Expert view**    Harriet Lake, Senior Business Development
Manager - Litigation and Investigations at Allen &
Overy, based in London, UK:

*"I received plenty of great advice from my then-boss, who was a Director at the time and is now a CMO. One thing that stands out is that she flagged the famous Harvard Business Review article entitled 'Management Time: Who's got the monkey? Initially published in 1974 on delegation, time management, and power politics. Management Time: Who's Got the Monkey? There are certainly a few outdated elements (and the feeding or shooting analogy is a bit much, poor monkeys). Still, the overall concept stuck with me, and I think it is beneficial in a professional services environment.*

*The lesson I took was always to be as mindful as possible about who I 'pass monkeys' to (both in the context of projects but also everyday tasks). Also, trying to rely on my initiative as much as possible/appropriate - have I taken this as far as I can myself? Is this the right person to handle? Do I need this person's input? Should I be dealing with the 'monkeys' I currently have, and if not, how do I fix that? I found it helpful at that time in my career, and I've never forgotten it.*

*It is helpful to reflect on when you start to manage people; it helps to keep everyone empowered and solutions-oriented, but it's also beneficial when considering your interactions with partners or your manager too."*

## Develop a sponsor for advancement

It is vital to identify key stakeholders that can help you progress your career advancement in your firm. With the proper planning and investment on your part, you can develop a strong relationship that can lead to career success for the both of you.

This sponsor can be someone that is considerably more senior than you or, if they sit within marketing, someone that leads a particular specialism in the firm that has the role you want in your career.

Consider what you want them to help you achieve. More importantly, determine how you provide value to your potential sponsor to ensure you create a two-way relationship, whether through your technical capabilities to support the stakeholder, knowledge of a specific sector, or help them with their objectives. Keeping your sponsor-supported will make you an even more appealing professional for your sponsor to support your advancement through the firm.

Take on broad initiatives across the firm or seek out specific stakeholders to make sure you stand out to potential sponsors who can support your firm's advancement.Cultivating these relationships with stakeholders takes time, so it is never too early to start such a process. The more visibility and trust you develop with this person, the more they will support your career at your firm.

> ▶ **Key points to remember**
>
> 1. Treat and communicate how your firm handles its meaningful external client relationships with your internal stakeholders.
>
> 2. Identify which stakeholders are critical to your promotion prospects and prioritise your energy and efforts in their direction.
>
> 3. When presenting to senior stakeholders to determine the challenges you are solving, define success and what decisions you need to make?
>
> 4. Focus on helping your manager succeed in their role through understanding their goals and how you can add value

# PART FIVE

## Proactive career management

*"Plans are only good intentions unless they immediately degenerate into hard work"*
*—Peter Drucker*

A key element in advancing your career is continuous personal development by remaining curious and open-minded, allowing you to develop yourself further. The professional services industry and the industries in which clients operate are constantly evolving, so you need to keep track of the latest developments to anticipate stakeholder needs internally and externally.

It is equally important to cultivate your external connections and manage your brand. There are times when you have to embrace an alternative route to advancement. Professional service Marketing teams have flat organisational structures, and newly created roles heavily depend on additional budgets or other factors. Therefore, you want to prepare for that eventuality by cultivating potential opportunities and preparing for your future.

In the industry, you will find that people talk. The community of colleagues feels smaller each year as you begin to build your network, meaning your professional reputation is paramount to cultivating opportunities. Increasingly, your peers' perception of you as a professional is more important than your technical skills or experience. People will always wonder if you will be able to handle varied types of situations and if you will be able to deal with a wide variety of people. Make sure to network with colleagues and peers, proactively look for such connections on LinkedIn, and attend professional service events to build and maintain relationships.

# 16

# Proactive Career Planning

*"Choose a job you love, and you will never have to work a day in your life"*
*—Confucius*

## Be more intentional with your career

In the professional services industry, you must build your career proactively to ensure positive career outcomes.

When settled into a role, it is all too easy to become complacent in your career advancement with just enough challenge and remuneration. It is not until you have reached a breaking point, disagree with the strategy, or can no longer advance professionally, that you are forced to assess your current position and whether opportunities exist outside your firm.

Without intentionality in planning, managing, and focusing your efforts, you will never receive the opportunities available to you in the industry.

**Expert view**   Deborah Macrae, Executive Professional Services Consultant and former BD & Market Director at some of Australasia's top tier law firms, based in New Zealand:

*"Proactive career management involves investing your time in a range of activities that allow you to achieve the career you want. These activities*

*include developing yourself, cultivating your external connections and managing your brand within the industry.*

*The day you stop learning is when you should think about doing something else!*

*A career in professional services can be gratifying but also extremely tough. Surround yourself with like-minded people. You will find you will often get your energy from your professional network. Using your network as a sounding board can constantly reassure you that you are not alone.*

*Make the time to invest in developing your professional network. It might take years to build "corporate currency" in the industry. Even if you don't leverage that network straight away, you will benefit throughout your career when you need it.*

*Enrol and participate in membership-based organisations, volunteer, further education, and attend events. All these practical activities will result in the growth of your professional network.*

*Managing your career development - Be curious! Ask open versus closed questions. Take an interest in what the technical staff do and how they will help you understand their drivers and challenges - allowing you to grow and develop your working knowledge.*

*Overall, it's crucial to have fun! So make sure you never lose your sense of humour."*

## Goal-oriented career planning

As with any strategy plan, you must decide on your objectives and determine how to achieve them. You need to pay attention to this regarding your professional development.

It would be best if you first determined your goals, such as gaining a position as Head of Brand at an international firm or a specialised role in branding, pitching, communications, or digital. Identifying this and retracing your steps is essential.

You operate in a market with many available positions to progress your career to where you want to be. The last few years have also taught us the importance of being more focused and mindful of our career development and broader growth than just salary and title. Thus it is crucial that you regularly self-reflect and question your current position and are you on track with your career direction.

## Expert view

Daniel Shaw, Director of Marketing & Business Development Recruitment (Professional Services) at Ernest Hunter Green, based in London:

*"How many times this week did you: learn, grow, succeed, feel inspired? Come on; you're at work for about 50+ hours a week, so you must be able to think of some examples. How about last month? Year? How many times this week did you get frustrated, complain, give up? List all the positive experiences on the right-hand side of the page. Then list all the negative ones on the left-hand side of the page. Done correctly, this reflects your career at this point.*

*That's where 'Career Mindfulness' comes in, which involves learning to channel your work expectations to the point where you have a clearly defined and tangible set of criteria for what you want out of your current (or next) job.*

*Your career has most likely taken steps that your education or career planning did not account for when you started. You must regularly take the time along the way to stop to think about what technical skills do you excel in? Are you a good communicator? What do people turn to you for advice about? What projects do they always ask you to take on? What do you avoid because you know you need to improve?*

*These themes will be prevalent throughout your career, irrespective of which particular company and job title you currently occupy. You should be mindful of them in the same way you are aware of your mental and physical wellbeing. Career Mindfulness is a way of being vocationally self-*

*aware, looking after yourself and making the right choices, at the correct times, throughout your career. Which, let's face it, is what you spend half your life doing and is what pays for you to have another half of life during the evenings and weekends! So it's worth your investment.*

*Career Mindfulness is all about applying that practice to your job and work environment. It's about calmly acknowledging your feelings and thoughts about your job and the environment that you base yourself in for all those hours every week. It's about looking at those two columns of positive and negative career weight and deciding if you are happy with your lot or want to move on and lose some of that weight.*

*Implementing this approach will provide you with the framework to better evaluate your career and to take the negative emotion out of your day-to-day frustrations by syphoning them off. Helping you assess whether you are in the right job or require a change to advance your career.*

*It's not a straight yes or no decision, but more of a percentage game. Everyone has different tolerances based upon different expectations and the compromises they are willing to make to meet them. But it is essential to be mindful of how your career is progressing. To recognise when you have slipped too far into the left column and taken decisive action to change jobs. Career Mindfulness is a constant process, not a case of binge and purge. It's a two-way flow of information and ideas. There are no shortcuts - not in the long-term."*

## Marketing, Business Development and Client Titles

There will be variations in titles and levels from firm to firm and around the world, although this is a valuable indication of the career steps to reach a specific position.

This list focuses on BD, marketing, and client titles. Of course, there are other areas in firms such as bid, communication, CRM, design, event, and digital marketing roles. Most of these have similar progressive levels as you move from junior positions to more senior roles.

You should identify your current level and the required levels to progress to your desired title in this list below.

To note, different firms have different title structures. For example, many US law firms or large international firms don't follow the traditional Assistant, Executive, or Senior Executive titles. Instead, they have titles such as Coordinator, Adviser or Specialist.

## Business Development

These roles focus on a mix of sales support and full-mix marketing activities, working closely with partners and junior advisors to put together strategic plans and advise them on targeting potential clients. Then work with the advisors to implement the strategy in collaboration with a wider Marketing team through cross-selling and client initiatives, bids, and events.

- BD Director
- Head of BD
- Senior BD Manager
- BD Manager
- Senior BD Executive / Coordinator
- BD Executive/Coordinator
- BD Assistant
- BD Administrator

## Client Relationship Manager

In these roles, you are responsible for managing client relationships and supporting the partners to maintain and grow business from the firm's most important clients. These roles can be far more strategic, with plenty of analysis, reporting and client feedback. Not many firms have dedicated client-focused roles, but this is an area where firms continue to recruit in.

- Head of Client Relationships

- Senior Client Relationship Manager
- Client Relationship Manager
- Senior Client Relationship Executive
- Client Relationship Executive

## Marketing

In a full-mix marketing role, you will often be involved in communications, digital, events, email marketing, and large-scale campaigns. Often you will also be involved in marketing analytics. You can promote the firm and your stakeholders as thought leaders in their fields of expertise through articles and opinion pieces, often as part of a fully integrated campaign.

- Head of Marketing / Marketing Director
- Senior Marketing Manager
- Marketing Manager
- Senior Marketing Executive
- Marketing Executive / Coordinator
- Marketing Assistant
- Marketing Administrator

## Career roadmap

Using LinkedIn, you can get an idea of the required skills and experience for each position you target. If possible, you should build a relationship with a few recruitment agencies in the professional service industry. By assessing the competencies and experience needed for such roles, you will obtain a clearer picture.

Find several people in these roles on LinkedIn to connect with and ask for their time to discuss their role and career advice, more often than not, most will be willing to share some guidance - I should know having asked numerous experts to contribute to this book. They might continue to mentor you as you progress in your career to prepare you for such a role if they are willing to help you get where you want to go.

## Developing the right skills and behaviours

In reviewing the list of manager-level roles and beyond, the following are the most frequently referenced skills and behaviours for success in these positions:

- excellent stakeholder management skills with the ability to build strong relationships at all levels.
- strong commercial acumen
- Deadline-driven and results-oriented, with strong project management skills.
- the ability to effectively prioritise work
- experience of line management (desirable)
- solutions driven
- a lateral thinker - identifies linkages and critical themes and is prepared to think differently about approaches to delivery.
- a continuous improvement approach
- exceptional communication and presentation skills
- proactive and acts on its initiative to devise creative solutions to complex problems.
- robust and resilient, with a positive, can-do attitude.
- ability to work autonomously as well as part of a team
- research-biassed and analytical mind

The list is not exhaustive but serves as a guide; when you think about your areas of strength and weaknesses, as you read through this book, we have covered specific strategies to improve your skills in these areas, both in your current position and in your career. Furthermore, The Chartered Institute of Marketing (CIM) has a framework that provides a guide (Professional Marketing Competencies) to the skills and behaviours expected of professional marketers at varying proficiency levels.

Your brand is more than a reflection of who you are today; it's a roadmap of where you want to go. After reviewing the list above, you should answer the following questions:

- What skills and competencies am I particularly strong in?
- What skills and competencies do I need to improve on?
- What skills are missing? What skills would I like to build but have not yet had the opportunity to practice?

It is a good idea also to define your career goals, so you know where you want to advance your career in the future. But the strategy (or strategies) you need to get there is the biggest challenge. To progress your career into senior positions, you must first embrace specific behaviour patterns and ways of performing your job that position you not just for senior positions but also the responsibility associated with senior positions.

**Expert view**    Keith Hardie, Partner at MD Communications and former Director of Innovation Marketing and BD at Bryan Cave Leighton Paisner LLP, based in London:

*"One thing that I think almost everyone does early in their career is identifying people they admire who are doing jobs that they would like to do in the future.*

*My advice is to list out the skills, capabilities, and experience these people have and then review your background to identify which elements you think you can offer and which you can't yet demonstrate. It sounds straightforward, but it can be very effective.*

*For most people, if they are honest with themselves, there will be a long list of things that they don't have. Even if they think they can do the job, they may not demonstrate this to a prospective employer, so thinking about 'how would I show I can do it in an interview' ahead of time is worth doing. Most people realise that if they were on the other side of the discussion, they might not convince them in many areas.*

*If you are early in your career, you should find lots of things that you need more experience of before you'll be ready for your ultimate job, and the idea is to find opportunities to fill those gaps. Each project, job or role you take on should be contributing to filling those gaps and providing you with examples of how you've delivered in each area.*

*Using this framework, you can consider each job you take and means that, even if a job doesn't seem to be what you want, you can see the positives and focus on learning from the experiences. It also means you can evaluate each opportunity and decide if it is taking you in the right direction or look for additional projects or responsibilities to focus on for your career development.*

*In addition, when you gain more experience, you find there is more to what looked simple than you expected!*

*In applying this simple approach, there are a few things to remember.*

1. *The skills you need are constantly changing. When I started my career, I worked with a typing pool (a secretary who typed out your hand-written scribbles) and printed out labels to post press releases; fax machines were considered relatively advanced! So don't just look up to people at the end of their careers. Think about new tools you need to understand and assess the techniques that those younger than you are applying successfully. I've learned a lot from brilliant young digital marketing experts within my teams. I paid for myself to do Google's digital marketing qualification because I recognised that it was an area where I lacked understanding.*

2. *Never see your plan as a straight jacket. The idea is to grow, but you may open doors you've previously never thought of trying. My original goal was to head up large communication teams, and I have been lucky enough to lead functions with up to 90 professionals. Still, along the way, I gained experience of launching over half a dozen legal start-ups, where I often didn't have a team at all, and I loved that too, so my ambitions have changed over time.*

3. *As you develop, don't try just to become a version of someone else. Bring together your own unique set of skills and experiences. So, as well as developing my marketing skills, I've got an MBA and training in PRINCE project management, Lean Six Sigma and Design Thinking. Combined with my marketing experience, I think this gives me a unique perspective and isn't one I think my early role models would have been able to offer."*

## Upskilling and reskilling

Whilst all firms should have plans for upskilling and reskilling in place for you, this is not true for all firms and does not reflect the many marketing professionals such as yourself who must take upskilling into your own hands. If you're taking a proactive approach to your professional development, the following suggestions may help:

- **Identify free or low-cost training and certification programmes** - there is a vast range of training and certification programmes available for marketers in the UK, from university degrees to quick, free online courses. For example, at the beginning of 2020, I underwent a KAM course for less than £50, presented by Professor Malcolm McDonald. These types of courses would usually cost more than a few thousand. These are an excellent way to add further credentials to your CV; for those who did a Marketing degree over ten years ago, this is a perfect way to learn in new marketing areas.

- **Digital marketing professionals should look to Google for training and certification** - with Google Analytics and Google Ads key programmes to have under your belt. Meanwhile, Hubspot Academy offers a range of entirely free marketing courses, including training focused on inbound marketing, content marketing, social media and email marketing. The lessons are bite-sized (some take no more than two hours), so while they may not be in-depth, they are easy to consume and absorb and can help develop new skills or polish existing ones.

- **International membership organisations** - Legal Marketing Association (LMA), Professional Services Marketing Group (PSMG), and Association of Accounting Marketing (AAM) are fantastic resources in terms of networking with peers, educating, and training.

- **Subscribe to the right publications** - marketing is ever-changing, which means marketers need to keep up with trends, developments, new technologies and best practices to stay ahead of the curve. Podcasts can be a goldmine for marketing news and conversation if you're more of an auditory learner. There is an array of available resources that have become available for you to utilise as part of your career development. I have collated a list of my recommendations. *[see BONUS MATERIAL]*

- **Explore mentoring and shadowing** - it can prove invaluable in showcasing the practical elements of a job, whether that's in a structured, formal capacity or more casual and ad-hoc. For example: over the last year, I mentored a Legal Technologist in our firm's IT team to be more client-facing and helped them commercialise a lot of the IT solutions they had been developing. I benefited from the process also as a mentee, learning a lot about this side of the business.

Mentors don't have to come from inside your organisation - consider reaching out to someone you admire in the industry or asking your employer, peers or friends if they know of anyone who might be interested in mentoring you.

You will find out more information about various resources that will help you upskill yourself, help your career and help perform to a high standard in your role. *[see BONUS MATERIAL]*

**Expert view**   Annette Morgan, Assistant Director - Major Events at EY, based in London:

*"Peer-to-peer mentoring has been a critical component of my development journey. When I met my former colleague Nicola, we immediately bonded over our similar work ethic and shared passion for our careers. We started having bi-weekly calls dedicated to setting goals, encouraging one another and importantly, holding each other accountable. We have shared job opportunities, read industry books together and sharing best practices for the past ten years.*

*Peer-to-peer mentoring has kept me on my toes. I want to come to meetings with fresh ideas, inspiring me to stay on top of industry news, attend conferences to gain new insights, and participate in industry forums. These help me develop a more well-rounded view of crucial topics like sustainability and technology. Having a peer who opens up opportunities for me by recommending jobs and pushing me to apply for mentoring or other industry schemes has been a real driver in my personal development. I feel that sharing our successes serves as a healthy motivator to one another to keep moving forward."*

## Developing a career across borders

Before the pandemic, I regularly saw firms send their marketing professionals on secondment to work in different jurisdictions. These are great opportunities to build up an international mindset and experience career opportunities around the globe.

Changing clients' demands, employee expectations, rapid technology developments, and other external factors will change the nature of career opportunities and access to global talent. A move to remote and hybrid working will allow you to work in international firms from any jurisdiction you reside in.

---

## Expert view

Hugo Pena, Director Of Business Development at Gonzalez Calvillo, based in Mexico City:

*"Developing a career across borders can be both a challenging and rewarding part of your career journey. In my career, I moved from Mexico to the UK, worked across Europe, then joined a US firm, and now back in Mexico. I learnt several nuances and critical lessons from working across different markets and would recommend those professionals in the industry looking to work in either the US, UK or other critical markets for professional services marketing should be aware of:*

*For over five years, I had the opportunity to lead efforts for a US firm with operations in the UK and then across Europe. I managed and led numerous business development initiatives and implemented action points daily. I became aware of the intricacies of each location, team, practice area and language.*

*I worked across different time zones and with varying mechanisms of reporting. There is a high level of responsibility and expectation of how effective you can be with the available tools. Proactiveness is everything.*

*Working as a non-native English speaker in the UK meant I had to prove myself twice – as hard. Many can relate to this statement. However, I was privileged enough to be part of a team in London that embraced cultural nuances in such a way that it added value. I brought -not only culturally but also because of my legal background - to contribute significantly. Incorporating such differences meant my skills had a platform to proactively develop strategies that perhaps I would not have developed back home.*

*Over the last decades, both the US and UK were the markets paving the way for business development and marketing professionals. Now other consolidated hubs are being created through clients' demands due to globalisation, which means you can seek out opportunities in other regions, sectors, and industries when proactively planning your career.*

*Embrace your uniqueness whilst reinventing yourself now and then. Keep a go-getter mentality, and the rest will follow suit."*

---

## Knowing when and how to move on in your career

You've been at your firm for quite a while, and you've noticed your motivation is waning. You could be feeling unchallenged or not moving in the direction you want your career to go.

It is usual for your interests and goals to evolve, but how can you determine when it is the appropriate time to change firms to pursue career advancement elsewhere? Now might well be the perfect time, if you notice these signs:

- **The "job" feels like a "job"** - when your current role no longer makes you happy, you may need a change. Although it is normal to feel frustrated with your job from time to time, when the negatives overpower the positives, it is time to consider whether another job is better suited for you.

- **Have trouble feeling challenged** - this could be a sign that you have achieved everything you can from your current position. If you think your work is routine and hasn't been exciting for you, a role change is required. Whenever you begin a new job, there are many new things to learn - new systems, new ideas, and new people. Over time, however, these things fade away, and you may not know as much. If you're not learning, it's time to move on.

- **A blocked route or stalled career progression** - motivation in any role comes from the feeling of working towards the next level. It might be time for you to look at more challenging roles that feel more worthy of your skills if the promotion doesn't seem possible because the next step up is blocked by your manager, or you applied internally but were unsuccessful.

- **Your perception of the firm has changed** - when you first joined, it seemed filled with possibilities, and you were proud to identify yourself as part of the firm. But this has changed for specific reasons, e.g., change in the atmosphere at the office, your belief in the organisation has diminished, and you disagree with recent commercial or strategic decisions. Your firm may not be making progress in critical areas such as diversity & inclusion or ESG.

**Expert view**  Hannah Taylor, Manager, Professional Services Marketing Recruitment at Carter Murray, based in London:

*"This is something I see regularly when placing senior and mid-level professionals in roles in the industry. Knowing when to move on from your current job can be a challenging decision that requires careful planning and a proactive approach.*

*Avoid comparing your progress to others. In all our careers, regardless of industry, we will have peers who do a similar job; however, every individual will have strengths and areas of improvement that play out in their career and impact the overall career path people take.*

*Everyone is different, and therefore your career choices and aspirations will be too. Take the time to think about your key strengths and critical areas for improvement. Focus on the areas that you enjoy or where you have core strengths. Decide where you require more support from your manager or further training and development on areas for improvement – helping you shape your own decisions on the next steps in your career.*

*Once you have identified what next steps you would like to take in your career, don't assume that it will happen overnight or that it will happen at your current organisation; speak to your manager and the senior leadership team at your firm about what you would like to do – helping you gain insight into what opportunities are available internally and shape your decision on what roles you would like to take. They can also give you insights into what external networks and connections they have or introduce you to help build external relationships.*

*If you identify there are no options internally, and require external support, speak to a trusted recruiter who is an expert in the area. They can give you an overview of the market, the salaries and skill sets required. They can also advise you on what seminars and networks to join or qualifications to take to add to your applications and general development.*

*When interviewing for new positions, follow the below guidance:*

- *Say 'I' rather than 'we' to ensure the interviewer can extract what it was that you did rather than the team.*

- *Give enough depth and detail to your answers– think about the STAR technique: Situation, Task, Action, Result for competency questions to ensure you give context to your answers.*

- *Research the company in-depth– not just the website– look at the clients and market intel relevant to the clients/sectors that the company focuses on so you can think about the challenges the client will be facing to help identify solutions.*

- *If you do not have experience in an area on the job description – ensure you demonstrate how you would go about approaching it – a lot of the time, it is more about your approach and how you think than having covered everything before.*

- *Think about what you would do in the first 90-days; this demonstrates to the interviewer you have thought through what it would be like in the role and how you would approach it.*

- *Ask relevant questions to understand the role and challenges faced by the team, rather than focusing on hours and pay– this helps to focus your interest in the role's responsibilities and overall opportunity.*

- *Ensure you proactively give examples in your answers and discussion points. Don't assume to be asked specific questions on areas – if you proactively discuss detailed competency answers, you will be able to show you have read the job spec and have thought through your relevant expertise.*

- *Do prepare for open questions such as, 'tell me about yourself?' These sets of questions can surprise you if you are expecting a competency-based interview.*

- *Try not to waffle and go off-topic- practising and preparing ahead can help focus your thoughts and answers to avoid this.*

- *Take the time to listen and then respond once you have had time to think about your answer - it is ok to have silence; this will show you are getting your thoughts together and will be much clearer if you give yourself time rather than diving straight in.*

- *As always, consider your skills and experience and how they transfer to the role you're interested in."*

---

➡️ **Key points to remember**

1.  Determine your career goals and what type of role you want to be in the future

2.  Use the job title list to identify your current and required levels to progress to your desired title.

3.  Find 1-2 people in these roles on LinkedIn and ask for their time to discuss their role and career advice.

4.  Review the various ways to upskill your expertise

# 17

# Personal development

*"They say Rome wasn't built in a day, but I wasn't on that particular job"*
*—Brian Clough*

## Knowledge acquisition

If you want to become an expert in specific fields during your career or become dependable internally in these fields, you will need to acquire knowledge continuously. Just as your firm's clients hire experts in your firm to assess a current problem and then create action plans for improvement, your internal stakeholders will expect the same from you.

During the early stages of your career, you likely focused on developing technical expertise in various marketing and business development areas. If this is your first role within the field, you must build a comprehensive understanding of the professional services industry [see **CHAPTER 1**]. It will help you develop basic knowledge of how to perform your role if you understand the dynamics, how marketing is delivered, and some of the key players in the market.

There is no way you can know everything about everything. Work and the professional services industry are constantly evolving due to several factors, including technological advances and changing jobs, new employee expectations and hybrid remote working. Monitor for new developments and learn more about topics you lack in knowledge.

Understanding your firm's products and services and how they help clients is crucial to a successful marketing campaign. The services firms in this industry are highly technical and complex, making this an extremely challenging task. To do this successfully, you shouldn't need to know about these topics to the extent where you can advise on them. Instead, identify the key issues, how the product solves them, and what it does, the decision making process a client would need to go through before buying. By doing this, you'll be able to determine the value proposition that your firm offers clients and help guide your marketing approach.

## Areas to focus on

Review your knowledge of the following areas to determine where you have specific gaps that require you to develop your understanding further:

- **Knowledge of your firm** - are you familiar with your firm's different products and services? Which clients are the most important? Locations? Strategy? Mission, values, and culture?
- **How well do you know your industry** - general economics? What are the key developments impacting the industry? Competition? Impact on society? Are technology developments taking place?
- **Key clients for your firm** - who are they? What is the decision-making process? Who are certain products targeting? In what ways do current trends impact them? Brand perception?
- **Technical topics** - what are the critical areas of your firm's work? Want to develop further?
- **Marketing specific** - what are your preferred marketing channels? Your expertise in particular areas such as (CRM), digital marketing, content marketing, and more.

For a list of recommended books in various fields to supplement your reading of this book. [see **BONUS MATERIAL**]

## Experience database

Working in the professional services industry is fast-paced. You will be involved in several marketing initiatives and gain exposure to a wide range of experiences that will position you well for future senior roles.

The challenge when work is fast-paced and the weeks blur by is that it can be tough to recall what you did last month, let alone a year ago. It makes it difficult to submit your promotion application, update your CV for a move elsewhere, or plan for your next appraisal. To avoid this, you need to build your very own experience database.

In the same way, your firm likely has developed credential lists of experiences that showcase their most outstanding work and expertise in certain areas. You should begin tracking key initiatives you are involved in, successful outcomes, other achievements and experience into a platform of your choice, whether a simple Word document or Excel sheet. You can download the template I use. **[see BONUS MATERIALS]**

Then when you have your next appraisal, need to update your CV or apply for a new position, you can turn to this helpful resource and recall essential information that will help you advance your career.

## Develop the fundamentals

Starting early in your career, you will develop technical expertise in marketing, business development, communications, events, and others. In helping you develop a strong understanding of these activities, it is vital that will allow you to make better decisions and when to utilise these as you move into senior roles. Often juniors can move into specialist areas that limit the types of opportunities available to your career because you have focused on developing knowledge and skills in a specific area.

## Specialisation and upskilling

When you advance into senior roles, you'll discover that you like certain aspects of your job, which will force you to seek out more specific functions such as client development, pitching, client communication and other areas. At this stage, you can begin to consider developing a deep technical understanding.

If you are interested in specialising in your career, you should be aware of the following challenges:

- **There is no clear path** - to reach a senior position in a specialist field, you are responsible for developing the skills and knowledge required for specific future jobs.
- **Training and development** - firms' approach to training and skill development is limited to mandatory and regulatory training.
- **Lack of knowledge** - lack of credentials and the knowledge you have acquired academically is often broad and can quickly become out of date in an evolving environment.

### In practice

My career has transitioned from focusing on using my marketing and business development expertise in broad roles to utilising them in a more focused sector marketing role. I have recently specialised in client development roles, building on my comprehensive understanding of the various fundamental skills and areas of knowledge required to operate in these positions successfully. When developing and planning my career, I have always found it helpful to reflect on my professional identity.

To help me focus on uncovering my skills and strengths, knowing these has allowed me to maximise these to develop my professional brand. The following questions should help you reflect on your brand:

- In which areas of work do I excel?

- What specific tasks motivate me?
- What characteristics have others complimented me on?
- Which tasks have others had to help me with repeatedly?
- When working on a team, what roles do I seek to fulfil?
- Which roles/tasks seem to drain my energy?
- Which tasks can I spend hours on without feeling overwhelmed or tired?

## Becoming a specialist

Marketers of tomorrow must adapt to the changing landscape of the industry - which requires you to build knowledge of these areas and implement it in your role. Upskilling also represents a cultural shift in the workplace as the workforce embraces more modern and forward-looking methods for client-centric marketing.

Therefore, you can thrive in your current role and develop future career prospects by investing your time in upskilling yourself. Developing your career in the right direction requires you to strategically identify and focus on the areas of upskilling that you should explore.

- **Roadmap** - using LinkedIn and industry-specific, you must prepare job boards, review jobs you are interested in and note the responsibilities and requirements. By comparing how you compare to these, you can identify areas for improvement.
- **Job shadowing** - try to schedule a meeting with someone who holds these types of positions within your firm so that you can learn more about what they do, how they got there, and how you can start working toward this type of position. You should try to find initiatives where you will be able to work closely with them to gain knowledge and experience about what their job involves.
- **Mentoring** - mentoring can prove invaluable in showing the practical aspects of a job, whether it's a structured, formal arrangement or more casual and ad-hoc. Your mentor does not have to come

from within your company. People are more accessible than ever through social media, and often people like to be engaged with and sought for their expertise. Reach out to someone you look up to or ask your colleagues, friends or employers to suggest someone who might be interested in mentoring you.

- **Knowledge acquisition** - the best way to acquire additional specialist knowledge on a topic is to deep dive into it. For example, if you are trying to understand new areas of marketing, such as account-based marketing (ABM), make sure to add the top three books to your Amazon wish list. In addition, if you prefer to watch or listen to content rather than read, LinkedIn Learning, YouTube, and other sources are helpful. I recently did a course on Udemy on this topic to develop my understanding of this area.

- **Training and credentials** - there are a wide variety of training and certification programmes available to marketers worldwide, ranging from university degrees to short, free online courses, to help you acquire credentials in specific topic areas needed to succeed in your current and future roles.

Most essential to highlight is that accumulated knowledge is only part of the process. Making your time investment all the more worthwhile is to test, pilot, teach others, implement the ideas and know-how you discover, and bring it into your role and firm.

---

**Expert view**     Eva Wisnik, Founder of Wisnik Career Enterprises, has placed more than 1,000 law firm business professionals into law firms since 1996. She is the author of "Your Fairy Job Mentor's Secrets for Success" and a frequent speaker at industry conferences, based in New York:

---

*"I want to share with you what thousands of law firm Marketing Directors and CMOs had told me when they tasked me with filling roles at their*

*firm, and what their top performers do that inspires their confidence and makes them stand out. Also, the critical mistakes professionals make that result in the loss of opportunities.*

*The truth is, what your boss will appreciate most of you boils down to your ability to get the right stuff done efficiently and on time - requiring competencies such as thinking proactively, taking the initiative, using good judgement and working hard.*

*Here's what you need to do to be a superstar contributor at work, build a strong reputation and be top of mind as new opportunities arise. Great news, you have the potential to master all of them!*

*Be self-driven - those internally driven and motivated to do a great job regardless of external carrots or recognition stand out to "bosses." These top performers measure their success by contributing to the team and learning in the process.*

*Execute and get things done efficiently - this trait is all about delivering desired results on time. These team members have strong organisational and time management skills, and they know how to use technology to maximise their efficiency.*

*Utilise practical intelligence - knowing things does not automatically make you a good problem solver who will achieve the results your boss needs. These star employees focus on getting the most important things done, and they are practical problem solvers and are results-driven.*

*Have situational awareness - the best contributors can size up situations and people and then adjust their work style and communications to meet the situation/person where they are. Their ability to "read the room" and use good judgement inspires trust.*

*Have (appropriate) self-confidence - these professionals have self-awareness and know their strengths and weaknesses. They believe in their ability to accomplish goals and have the courage to take on projects in new areas. Yet, they know what they don't know and overstate their abilities and lose credibility.*

**Key points to remember**

1. Review the "areas to focus" section and identify where you have specific knowledge gaps

2. Create and start capturing your experience and successful outcomes in an "experience database."

3. Identify specific areas you enjoy doing the most in your current role and would like to do more of, then identify what specialised senior positions will allow you to do this in the future.

4. Seek out training, mentorship, and job shadowing to develop further expertise in the areas you want to grow.

# 18

# Maximising performance appraisals

*"You can't manage what you can't measure"*
*—Peter Drucker*

## Understanding the importance of appraisals

This part should be relatively easy for you if you have successfully applied many of the behaviours discussed throughout this book and executed more strategic behaviours in your role.

If you're like most people, appraisals are something you often dread, which results in you going into them thinking defensively, feeling insecure, and expecting conflict. Rather than seeing your appraisal as a chore, you should understand that it is your chance to progress your career; this is why going about it the right way will result in significant benefits for you.

As your manager often has several appraisals to conduct, they may not recall every achievement or key highlight since your last appraisal, so you must prepare as much as possible before the meeting. If you have created an "experience database", review it to find out what you have been focusing on lately and any successful outcomes you want to highlight during your discussion.

It may be the case that your performance has not been that impressive during the recent period, either because of poor performance on a specific objective or lack of results on a particular initiative. You should not avoid discussing these topics; instead, take the initiative to bring them up. Doing it this way will show initiative to your manager since they may not have known how to raise the issue. It is essential to be honest about your performance and where you have failed. It is also necessary to demonstrate what you have learned and how your manager can help you. It may be that your objectives are unrealistic or need more support, or you need to reprioritise your time to make sure that you allocate more time to these objectives.

In the appraisal, you want to have an end goal in mind: what are you hoping to accomplish or cover in the process? Consider various options, such as promotion, more training, or a pay raise, and plan the conversation accordingly. The key to unlocking your future ambitions is preparing yourself to make a case for why they are important to you and how they will help you grow the firm in your role at the firm.

It's essential to take advantage of your opportunity when undertaking an appraisal with your manager. It allows you to get meaningful feedback and guide you in the right direction.

## Preparing for your appraisal

To get formal feedback, use your firm's internal feedback process or reach out directly to your vital internal stakeholders a few weeks before the meeting. Review and compile before your appraisal. The purpose of this is to understand your performance from the viewpoint of your peers and stakeholders. You should send your feedback ahead of the meeting so your manager can see it.

Before the meeting, make sure you review your goals and progress toward them. Additionally, it is essential to check recent activities and examples of success, including marketing initiatives that led to new clients or positive client engagement.

This stage is where you should invest your time gathering evidence of all you have done for your firm. Focus on highlighting the results of your work and their worth to your firm.

## Expert view

Verity Jackson-Grant, Head of Marketing & Business Development - Pricing at Simmons & Simmons, based in London:

*"Don't spring a promotion request on your manager at appraisal time or be disappointed if not rewarded with a promotion without making it clear that that is your goal.*

*Engage your manager and senior stakeholders in conversations about your future and ask them what they think you need to do or show to move to the next level. Proactively seek opportunities that will enable you to demonstrate your skill set and how you have developed, and collect evidence and real-time feedback as you go rather than in the days before the meeting. Bad managers might feel threatened by this approach, but good managers will encourage and support you.*

*Never be afraid to talk about money. Keep it professional, go prepared with a figure in mind and make sure you can articulate your reasoning, but don't shy away from the conversation. Most firms operate on the basis that you get what you're given, with many deciding on salary increases and bonus amounts before you've even had your appraisal with your manager. Still, there is often scope for negotiation for those brave enough to start the discussion.*

*Sometimes roles are malleable, which can be shaped to your skillset and sometimes you can create new positions. I explicitly developed my current role after putting together a job specification and a paper demonstrating the value I would bring to the firm if only I were given the opportunity."*

## Try finding areas to develop

In an appraisal, you can also determine what areas you need to improve to perform better and ultimately progress in your career. You and your manager can use your appraisal to discuss what needs to be developed and what specific resources are available to support you internally and externally.

Before your appraisal, identify the training and resources available to you, both internally and externally, and consider what the business case will look like - how will the firm benefit from funding you to enrol? After gaining this insight, how can you share it more widely?

## Looking ahead

Consider what tasks and objectives you need to focus on over the next few months. Ensuring you are focused on the right priorities and aligned with your manager's expectations. Put some thought into ways you can add additional value above and beyond your current responsibilities, such as:

- what marketing initiatives could you lead?
- what ideas do you have that could streamline the existing marketing processes?
- Additional training required to take on more responsibility?
- Create a specific plan for how you can solve problems in the firm
- Any other ideas you have that could help your firm and your clients

**➡️ Key points to remember**

1. Consider what you want to get out of your appraisals, such as promotion, more training, or a pay raise so you can plan accordingly.

2. Obtain feedback from your key stakeholders to understand how your performance is perceived

3. Review your goals and progress toward them. Consider the tasks and objectives you need to focus on over the next few months.

4. Before your appraisal, it is crucial to research external courses and resources that your manager could allocate to enrol in.

# 19

# Resilience and recovering from setbacks

*"It's just a flesh wound!"*
*—Monty Python and the Holy Grail*

## Importance of developing resilience

In today's career environment, gone are the times when you spend your entire career in the same firm, keeping your head down doing the same tasks and being promoted based on loyalty and length of service.

Instead, your career will likely make many changes due to the firm and market changes. Internal promotions and applying for external opportunities to progress your career are more competitive than ever.

Your career may face setbacks and frustration, whether you are unsuccessful in getting that promotion or for that new role at another firm that would have advanced your career.

As part of a successful career strategy and performing at a high level, you must develop resilience. Becoming more resilient is a behaviour you can learn and a way of working that will allow you to keep going and growing.

## Recovering back from setbacks

Changing roles may be necessary for advancement, whether it is to move into a more senior role, to earn a higher salary, or for another reason. It is often necessary to assess the risks of changing our career path when we move from one role to another. There are situations, however, where we may not be able to predict career mistakes until it is too late.

With the limited information we have, we make the most informed career decisions we can. No career decision can be predicted completely. As discussed, careers in the industry are no longer linear, and your career will likely appear chaotic on the surface with several role changes.

1. Allow yourself to forgive yourself and to let go of the guilt. It is easy to get caught up in regretting your decision and being harsh on yourself. However, you need to remember why you pursue the career move in the first place. Starting positions are always a gamble, and sometimes they don't work out. Acknowledging that it is time to improve your situation and move on. If you are hard on yourself, you could hinder your ability to create new opportunities.

2. Assess your options [see **CHAPTER 16**]. Develop a plan and determine your next step. Assess your next job, the role, culture, compensation, and other factors. Most likely these will be very different from your current position, which has proven to be a mistake. You made a mistake with your previous move, so identify the elements that are non-negotiable and don't settle for anything less. Making a rash decision to change roles to find out later that it is a mistake will only set you back.

3. Talk to a mentor, a friend, or a career coach about your goals. You should discuss your options with someone you trust, preferably someone who is unbiased and understanding of your situation. By discussing your situation with a mentor, trusted contact in your industry, friend, or even a career coach, you will gain a different perspective. You will discover options you had not considered. In those stuck moments, your vision narrows, your horizons shrink, and you miss obvious ways to move forward. Talking might just open up new avenues.

4. Get back on your feet. Update your CV, contact recruiters and begin applying for jobs.

Career moves aren't right or wrong, just choices, and they're not always ideal. What matters is how you respond and how you pursue new opportunities.

---

**Expert view**   Claire Rason, Founder at Client Talk Ltd and host of the podcast Lawyer's coach, based in Reading:

---

*"Resilience is often described as the ability to bounce back from tough life events. The first thing to note here is that they are "tough". Typically, you might feel emotions such as anger, sadness, or frustration. Resilience is moving past these emotions and carrying on towards achieving your career objectives.*

*As a coach, I am often called upon to support individuals in building resilience. They probably don't call it that, and they are more likely to say they are overwhelmed or stuck. The truth is many of us have stores of resilience that we perhaps aren't aware of or that we forget about when we need them most.*

*When you are in the middle of one of those times, it is hard to remember that you have all the tools at your fingertips to bounce back and stop.*

*Yes, stop.*

*Try and take a moment to breathe. Practice deep breathing for five and out for eight seconds. Repeat this a few times. When you start to feel more grounded, reflect on when you bounce back. Maybe it was a promotion that didn't go your way or a pitch that you lost after many late nights getting it over the line, or an experience that wasn't work-related at all. Think about what you did to bounce back. What resources did you utilise? Those resources might be internal, or they might be something like a friend who listened to you. What did you learn from that experience? Think about how those reflections might help you now. What could you draw on to move forward?*

*Resilience is something that all professionals build through overcoming experiences. That means going through tough times, and we don't talk about these times as much as we should as a society. If you are struggling to work out how your resilience stores could help you, why don't you enlist the help of a colleague? Why don't you find out when they went through a hard time at work and what they did and learnt from the experience? An eye-opening exercise, and done with empathy and kindness can build stronger bonds in teams too."*

## Recovering from a wrong career move

Sooner or later you might change roles to advance your career, whether it is to move into a senior role, higher salary or another reason. When we change roles in our career, we often have to assess the risks of making such a move, but often there are scenarios where we cannot foresee career mistakes until it is too late.

Often we make the best decision we can make for our career with the limited information we have. We can never totally foresee. As discussed, no longer are careers in the industry linear, and that your career will likely look chaotic on the surface with several role changes.

1. Acknowledge and free yourself of the guilt, you can get caught up in regretting your decision and being hard on yourself, but it is important you revisit why you pursue your career move. Accepting a new position is always a gamble, and sometimes it will just not work out. Recognising that it is obviously time to improve your situation and move on. Being hard on yourself will not help and could get in the way of you creating new opportunities.

2. Assess your options **[see CHAPTER 16]**. Make a plan and identify your next move. Reevaluate what your next role is, what the role, culture, compensation, and other factors need to be, likely these will be a contrast to your current role which has turned out to be a mistake. Having made a mistake with your last move, make

sure you identify what elements are non-negotiable and most importantly do not settle for anything less, making a rash move into another role to find out that is a mistake will only set you further back.

3. Speak to your mentor, friend or a career coach about what you are looking for. Talk through your options with someone you trust, ideally a person who is unbiased, yet who can view your situation with empathy. Talking about your situation with a mentor, trusted contact in your industry, friend or even career coach will give you a different perspective, and help you see options you had not seen before. When you are in that stuck place, your vision narrows, your horizons shrink, and you are likely to miss obvious ways to move forward. A conversation might just open new avenues.

4. Bounce back. Update your CV, connect with industry recruiters and begin applying for roles.

There is no right and no wrong career move, just choices, and they are not always ideal. But it's how you respond and seek new opportunities that is important.

---

**Expert view**    Jamie Wallis, Head of BD, International Corporate & Special Projects at DLA Piper, based in London:

---

*"I experienced this during my career when I quickly realised that my boss was not supportive of me challenging stakeholders at the firm I was working at. The culture at the firm viewed Marketing as "support", which indicated that my days were already numbered! I had to temper my approach, and I held back in sharing my opinion. Unsurprisingly, I became disenchanted very quickly and looked to move on.*

*But even that was a challenge; I had made a mistake and didn't want a CV filled with short stays at different firms. So I bided my time. I got a couple of offers but turned them down because whilst they might have improved what I was doing, my gut instinct told me it wasn't the right fit. There was no point in making two mistakes on the bounce. I was patient. Yes, I was unhappy, but I backed myself and knew the right opportunity would come along.*

*When it did (via my network, not an agency, interestingly), I moved to a firm where I spent several happy years and progressed my career.*

*My key learnings from all of this? I moved for the wrong reasons. I got caught up in the recruitment and interview process and failed to listen to my initial instincts. But – look at the positives. I learnt a lesson about the importance of culture, how important it was to have a boss/leader that backed and supported you, about biding my time and being transparent in my mind about what was important to me in my next role.*

*When I talked to others, I found out that many of us had made a poor move at some point. It's not the end of the world; it happens. But don't sit there and moan about it. Only you can fix it!"*

---

### ➡️ Key points to remember

1. As part of a successful career strategy and performing at a high level, you must develop resilience.

2. You will gain more resilience to similar situations that may arise in your career following career setbacks.

3. It is essential to distinguish between self-doubt of your ability and analysing specific areas to improve.

4. When presented with a setback, this is the opportune moment to review where you are and the opportunities to move forward. If you make a bad career move, it is important you bounce back.

# 20

# Establishing and managing your reputation

*"People need dramatic examples to shake them out of apathy and
I can't do that as Bruce Wayne. As a man I'm flesh and blood.
I can be ignored. I can be destroyed. But as a symbol,
as a symbol I can be incorruptible, I can be everlasting"*
*—Batman*

## Show what you know

The act of doing your job day after day as a specialist in your field is one thing; however, proving your expertise is quite another. I have come to understand the importance of developing your brand proactively through articles in industry publications, presentations at conferences, and podcasting only later in my career.

Identifying unique topics resulting from the challenges you face in your current role and pitching them to editors is relatively straightforward. Years ago, I would never have thought about doing this. The industry continues to face intense competition for both internal and external roles, so establishing your reputation is essential now, more than ever.

You don't need to overcommit; you are undoubtedly busy already; however, you should commit to completing one thought leadership activity per year, for example, an article published in a publication or internal training to colleagues.

## Expert view

Lindsay Griffiths, Executive Director at International Lawyers Network (ILN). She was awarded "Thought Leader of the Year" by the Legal Marketing Association's New York chapter in 2014, based in New Jersey:

*"When it comes to managing your career, it helps to be strategic in how you establish your reputation in the market, just as you help your firm do, in your role. First, identify your goal or goals – while you don't need to have your five-year plan written out, have a general idea of the type of work you'd like to be doing, the type of firm you'd like to work for, and the type of people you enjoy working with is helpful. Then, create a plan that identifies the strategies and tactics you'll use to get there and what type of reputation you need to develop to achieve these. What do you want to be known for? What expertise do you want to demonstrate externally?*

*There are as many ways to network today as there are people, so when you're developing your career plan, you don't have to force yourself to do too many things outside your comfort zone.*

*While it's always a good idea to at least try some things to see whether you'll enjoy them or not (writing, public speaking, etc.), if you hate something, there are better ways to leverage your skills. Choose the activities that you enjoy and excel at – if you're a great writer, try blogging and use this as a way to meet influencers in your industry by quoting them in a post. If you want to try your hand at podcasting, interview some of your lawyers as guests to highlight their expertise.*

*If you enjoy public speaking, work on perfecting your presentation style and volunteer to speak at events, connecting with audience members before and after. Each of these activities will build your brand on its own. Still, they're also an opportunity for you to create connections with people in the industry, particularly when you multiply your efforts by using social media to share posts, link to episodes, connect with attendees, and work to become a thought leader.*

*When you start with a goal in mind, the strategies and tactics that you should use to establish your reputation will become clear."*

---

## In practice

Since the beginning of the year, I set out to be published in several industry publications, appear in as many podcasts, and speak at an industry conference. After several months of proactively pursuing such objectives, I have achieved all of these activities.

Considering I had no external brand outside of my firm or LinkedIn connections, I proactively researched publications, podcasts and other related sector channels to identify who the editor/host is and any guidelines relating to their contributor guidelines.

I then compiled and kept a list of topics I thought others would find helpful. Often the inspiration for such issues came from me searching for insight or guidance into a particular point I was trying to overcome in my role and thought others might be facing a similar problem.

---

## Expert view
Dal Banwait, Clients & Growth Business Partner at KPMG, based in London:

---

*"The most fundamental personal development point I worked on in my career, and I feel, has served me well, was building my brand. As Marketers, we all know the power of Brand PR and Marketing and how it contributes immensely to the growth of a firm. So it's somewhat ironic that many of us forget the importance of pushing our brand. According to various studies, hiring managers report that a candidate's brand significantly influences hiring decisions. It's imperative, therefore, to spend some time on your brand image internally and externally.*

*First and foremost, though, be very clear on what your desired goal is. We all roll our eyes at that question, 'where do you see yourself in five or ten years, but it does help shape your career path if you have a clear vision in* advance. If you don't, you will likely wind up doing the same job for longer than you want to, or end up in 10 years, wondering how you are doing a job you don't want to do. So once you have a clear vision, start working on mapping out how you can get there and build in how you intend to grow your brand.

Astonishingly, the majority of jobs fill up through networking. One of the best things I did to build my brand, build my confidence and get noticed was externally, and it was one of the best but initially one of the hardest things to do. So to start, I used to go along to events hosted by my firm and speak to a few delegates.

I joined various business networks to promote my brand, look for business opportunities, or even get business cards to share with relevant partners to be proactive.

Sometimes it would lead to new work for the firm, and sometimes it wouldn't. The main thing was that I intended to help build the business and promote the firm. 'Support' is a term often used to describe professionals in the industry, which frustrated me, so I was keen to show I could contribute to the business. Again it's always tough to start with, but everyone has been in the same position. As I became more confident, I received invites to sit on committees and boards, which further expanded my brand outside my job and incidentally led to many job offers.

Another way to build your brand externally is to post and write. So, to begin with, you can do something as simple as writing posts or articles on the firm's intranet or similar channels at work. You can also re-share articles and posts from your firm to your network on social media. Once you get comfortable with this, you can start to write a few sentences to go alongside those posts you are sharing. Over time, you will get comfortable writing your posts. You could then explore writing short articles for relevant publications and ask your external PR team to advise on how to get these out into the market.

Be clear on your elevator pitch. We talk about the importance of describing a product or service in a few short words or even a concise value proposition in our jobs, but we are seldom good at doing this for ourselves. Have a few 30-60 second pitches pre-prepared in your back pocket that describe *your critical successes or something unique. About yourself, something you have done, are proud of or are doing. Think about what you want people to remember about you, what makes you stand out from the crowd.*

*Remember, building your brand does take time and effort. Be clear on how you want to be perceived and known. Invest in selectively engaging with projects, events, meetings, client meetings, and industry bodies, maximising interactions, all of which can help get you more recognised internally and externally in the market. You can strengthen your brand within months if you take one action each day, small or big. Remember, people that get promoted or achieve career success through new opportunities tend to be those that are not only visible in their firm but add value, are trusted and are seen as credible to the external industry."*

## Leveraging LinkedIn

You probably initially created a LinkedIn profile when applying for your first professional job and have not used it as an online CV. However, most of the benefits will come from using LinkedIn as part of your current career when you are employed. You can gain several benefits from LinkedIn:

- **Build and improve your external profile** - as covered earlier in the book, you should now understand the importance of using your LinkedIn profile to connect with your internal stakeholders and colleagues to use your profile to develop your internal reputation. It is also vital to use your profile to externally communicate to the industry and connections as to who you are and your expertise. Ensure you are active on LinkedIn and frequently post about industry developments and share key posts your firm's puts out.

- **Maintain and develop your connections** - the people you know from school, university, and your professional career can offer you and your firm. You can use LinkedIn as part of your CRM, making it a habit to connect with everyone you come across. You become part of their world once you are connected. You can follow, engage with their posts, and they will see what you share with them; this all builds awareness.

- **Plan for future roles and what you need to do to get there** - as you think long-term about where you want to be in the next five, ten and beyond years, it's essential to identify what might be and possible steps there. LinkedIn is an excellent tool for identifying those roles and learning more about the requirements of those roles. You can seek out people who hold these positions and make connections with them. Senior leaders are often willing to offer advice and support in the industry. Still, since they are busy professionals, you must consider what would be most helpful and not treat them as an on-demand resource.

---

### In practice

You've likely heard the familiar adage, *"it's not about what you know, but who you know"*. Networking within the professional services industry has certainly changed over the years; it's still just as important as ever, mainly as you spend more of your career working in the industry and developing your brand.

I often find that the new contacts I meet in the industry share mutual contacts that we have previously worked with throughout my career. The more senior you get in the industry, this is common.

When applying for a new role, your future line manager can informally get feedback on your past performance or attitude. Two recent examples to share:

- I came across a candidate that applied for a role I was recruiting. I saw that they had worked at a firm where I knew the CMO. I reached out to my contact for their informal feedback on whether the candidate was someone I should invite to interview.

---

She agreed it would be, so I followed their advice; this was more important than what was in their CV.

- When searching for candidates for another role I recently started recruiting for, I saw a candidate who had previously worked at their firm in their sector team. I called my former manager up and asked for their opinion.

These two stories showcase the importance of developing a positive brand image internally and externally. You never know when your former colleagues will discuss with you and consider you for future career opportunities in the industry.

## Learn from others

While you are building your network externally, you must effectively utilise this network to identify what others in the industry are doing to stay ahead of trends and overcome challenges. Whether you engage on LinkedIn or through external industry events, growing and regularly engaging with your contacts will give you a broader perspective than the priorities you may be working on today.

In this way, you will gain exposure to a range of different perspectives, experiences, and ideas that you would otherwise miss if you focused only on your internal network.

**Expert view**     Charlotte Sansom, Senior Communications & PR Manager EMEA & Asia-Pacific at a global law firm, based in London:

*"I genuinely believe that every day is a school day. No matter how senior you are, there is always something new to learn and learn from others. Marketing, business development, and communications practices are constantly evolving. Technology advancement, changes in the market*

*(COVID being an example of a disrupter), and client behaviour indicate that staying current and aware of new best practices is vital.*

*I don't think it is possible to overestimate the value of building connections and listening to*

*and learning from others. I feel hugely privileged to tap into the thinking of colleagues in the market whom I consider operating at the cutting edge of a particular aspect of marketing, business development and communications.*

*These connections help me enhance my practice and the value I can bring to my firm. In turn, and as a team leader, I welcome those who bring new and diverse insights from their learnings.*

*For example, investing my time to support others, whether as a manager, mentor, committee member, judge or assessor, has been hugely rewarding and led to learning and career opportunities I would never have predicted.*

*My advice would be to get involved and to connect with, listen to, and wherever possible to support others."*

---

 ## Key points to remember

1. Competition for roles in the industry is intensifying, so investing your time outside of work in developing your external reputation is crucial for career success.

2. Demonstrate your expertise to your network. Commit to producing thought leadership, whether in an article or appearing on a podcast.

3. LinkedIn is a powerful tool for building your external reputation, managing your network, and planning your future career route.

4. Utilise your network effectively so that you can identify what others in the industry are doing to stay ahead of trends and overcome challenges.

# CONCLUSION

## Putting it all together

*"Be not afraid of going slowly, be afraid only of standing still"*
*—Chinese Proverb*

You've just finished reading this book, and your head is swimming with ideas. You're probably wondering, Where do I begin?

### Where to begin

Now you should have a more in-depth understanding of how you can be more strategic with your career progression, think differently, take action. Be clearer on the various tools and processes you have read about in this book to develop yourself and your career.

Writing this book aims to produce an industry book that contains all the things you will need to consider and act upon whether you are starting your marketing career in the professional services industry or are currently working towards senior roles. In addition to my ideas and knowledge, I have sought out some of the most senior and experienced professionals worldwide to share their recommendations and insights.

As stated, the intention of this book is not to provide something you only read once. This book is your very own career manual, full of ideas and guidance to help you advance your career. Look upon this as a source of reassurance and inspiration when you feel stuck or have challenges you are trying to overcome to progress your career.

To help you get out there and begin using the guidance in this book, I suggest you review the key takeaways from each chapter and download the templates and additional materials that you can access for free, alongside the bonus chapter as mentioned in the introduction. **[see BONUS MATERIAL]**

Now is the time for you to self-reflect on your career to date, to determine which chapters you need to focus on implementing the ideas and guidance outlined in this book. Whether it is to be more purposeful and strategic with your career direction, work more effectively in a team, manage internal stakeholders and proactively manage your career.

You can contact me by email to: dominicayresbook@gmail.com or connect with me on LinkedIn (linkedin.com/in/dominicaayres) and Twitter (https://twitter.com/DominicAyres). I would like to hear how you have applied any of the ideas set out in this book in your role and career to help you advance your career.

Remember, the only person who will advance your career is you. I wish you all the best with your career journey and hope you find this book of great value in helping you create the career you want.

# References and acknowledgements

1. Admin (2014). How To Recover from a Bad Career Move. [online] Careers Enhanced. Available at: https://www.careersenhanced.com/how-to-recover-from-a-bad-career-move/ [Accessed 11 Dec. 2021].
2. ANTHEM (2021). Junior Guide to Legal Marketing and Business Development. [online] ANTHEM. Available at: https://anthemconsulting.co.uk/wp-content/uploads/BD-and-Marketing-Guide-PDF.pdf.
3. Arnold, T. and Tomlinson, G. (2008). The marketing director's handbook : the definitive guide to superior marketing for business and boardroom success. Marlow: Marketing Directors.
4. Berger, J., Cohen, B.P. and Zelditch, M.J. (2015). Status Characteristics and Expectation States. oaktrust.library.tamu.edu. [online] Available at: http://oaktrust.library.tamu.edu/handle/1969.1/154605 [Accessed 13 Dec. 2021].
5. CIM (2019). Professional Marketing Competencies | CIM. [online] Cim.co.uk. Available at: https://www.cim.co.uk/membership/professional-marketing-competencies/.
6. Collis, D. and Rukstad, M. (n.d.). Can You Say What Your Strategy Is? [online] Available at: https://www.wright.edu/sites/www.wright.edu/files/page/attachments/Can-you-say-what-your-strategy-is.pdf.
7. DAP. (2020). B2B and B2C Marketing: 6 Key Differences You Should Know. [online] Available at: https://www.digitalauthority.me/resources/6-main-differences-between-b2b-and-b2c-marketing/.
8. Forrester. (2020). Supercharging Sales with Dynamic Guided Selling. [online] Available at: https://www.forrester.com/blogs/supercharging-sales-with-dynamic-guided-selling/ [Accessed 17 Dec. 2021].
9. Gartner. (n.d.). Definition of Chief Marketing Officer (CMO) - Gartner Marketing Glossary. [online] Available at: https://www.

gartner.com/en/marketing/glossary/chief-marketing-officer-cmo-[Accessed 13 Dec. 2021].

10. Greene, J. and Greene, J. (2021). With salaries up to $1 million, law firm marketing pros finally get some respect. Reuters. [online] 6 Dec. Available at: https://www.reuters.com/legal/legalindustry/with-salaries-up-1-million-law-firm-marketing-pros-finally-get-some-respect-2021-12-06/ [Accessed 14 Dec. 2021].

11. Harvard Business Review. (1999). Management Time: Who's Got the Monkey? [online] Available at: https://hbr.org/1999/11/management-time-whos-got-the-monkey.

12. Harvard Business Review. (2014). Effective Marketing for Professional Services. [online] Available at: https://hbr.org/1984/09/effective-marketing-for-professional-services.

13. Johnson, J. (2017). Am Law 200 Marketing Leader Snapshot - Data on Tenure and Title. [online] Calibrate Legal. Available at: https://calibrate-legal.com/law-200-marketing-leader-snapshot-data-tenure-title/ [Accessed 13 Dec. 2021].

14. Keller, G. and Papasan, J. (2014). The ONE thing : the surprisingly simple truth behind extraordinary results. London: John Murray.

15. Larrick, R.P. 2004. Debiasing. In The Blackwell Handbook of Judgment and Decision Making. D.J. Koehler & N. Harvey, Eds. Oxford: Blackwell.

16. Leadership IQ. (n.d.). Types Of Power Quiz: Do You Use Referent Power, Reward Power, Coercive Power, Legitimate Power, Expert Power or Information Power? [online] Available at: https://www.leadershipiq.com/blogs/leadershipiq/types-of-power-quiz-do-you-use-referent-power-reward-power-coercive-power-legitimate-power-expert-power-or-information-power.

17. Levitt, T. (2015). Marketing Intangible Products and Product Intangibles. [online] Harvard Business Review. Available at: https://hbr.org/1981/05/marketing-intangible-products-and-product-intangibles.

18. Lincoln, J. (2017). 7 Tips To Be Successful As A New Marketing Manager. [online] Inc.com. Available at: https://www.inc.com/john-lincoln/7-tips-to-be-successful-as-a-new-marketing-manager.html?utm_source=pocket_mylist [Accessed 14 Dec. 2021].

19. Marketing Officer. (n.d.). [online] Available at: https://www.spencerstuart.com/-/media/2021/july/cmoplaybook/cmoplaybook.pdf?utm_source=pocket_mylist [Accessed 14 Dec. 2021].

20. Mckeown, G. (2014). Essentialism : the disciplined pursuit of less. New York: Currency, An Imprint Of Crown Publishing Group.

21. Mellers, B.A. & Locke, C.C. 2007. What have we learned from our mistakes? In Advances in Decision Analysis: From Foundations to Applications. W. Edwards, R.F. Miles, Jr & D. von Winterfeldt, Eds. New York: Cambridge University Press.

22. MindTools (2019). Developing Commercial Awareness: Understanding How Businesses Make Money. [online] Mindtools.com. Available at: https://www.mindtools.com/pages/article/developing-commercial-awareness.htm.

23. Murphy, M. (2012). The source and power of influence [Video file]. Available: https://www.youtube.com/watch?v=jvCNuHMOubk [2017, July 21].

24. PricewaterhouseCoopers (2019). The evolving role of the B2B CMO: Reclaiming the strategic high ground. [online] PwC. Available at: https://www.strategyand.pwc.com/gx/en/insights/2019/evolving-role-b2b-cmo.html#:~:text=Progressive%20companies%20are.

25. PushFar. (n.d.). Professional Career Progression - How To Get Ahead. [online] Available at: https://www.pushfar.com/article/career-progression/?utm_source=pocket_mylist [Accessed 14 Dec. 2021].

26. Sluss, D. (2020). Stepping into a Leadership Role? Be Ready to Tell Your Story. [online] Harvard Business Review. Available at: https://hbr.org/2020/04/stepping-into-a-leadership-role-be-ready-to-tell-your-story?utm_source=pocket_mylist [Accessed 14 Sep. 2021].

27. Smart Insights (2018). Choosing effective digital marketing KPIs | Smart Insights. [online] Smart Insights. Available at: https://www.smartinsights.com/goal-setting-evaluation/goals-kpis/choosing-effective-digital-marketing-kpis/.

28. The Decision Lab. (n.d.). Dunning - Kruger effect - Biases & Heuristics. [online] Available at: https://thedecisionlab.com/biases/dunning-kruger-effect/.

29. The evolving role of the B2B CMO Reclaiming the strategic high ground. (n.d.). [online] Available at: https://www.strategyand.pwc.com/gx/en/insights/2019/evolving-role-b2b-cmo/evolving-role-b2b-cmo.pdf [Accessed 17 Dec. 2021].

30. The Muse. (n.d.). 6 Ways to Prepare for Your (Someday) Promotion Now. [online] Available at: https://www.themuse.com/advice/6-ways-to-prepare-for-your-someday-promotion-now?utm_source=pocket_mylist [Accessed 24 Nov. 2021].

31. The Muse. (n.d.). There's No Such Thing as a Right Career Decision. [online] Available at: https://www.themuse.com/advice/no-really-why-there-are-no-right-or-wrong-career-decisions [Accessed 17 Dec. 2021].

32. Yolanda Cartusciello (2016). Chief Marketing Officer: The Law Firm Change Agent. [online] PP&C CONSULTING. Available at: https://ppandcconsulting.com/law-firm-culture/chief-marketing-officer-law-firm-change-agent/?utm_source=pocket_mylist [Accessed 14 Dec. 2021].

33. Wharton IDEAS Lab. (n.d.). Imposter Syndrome's Unexpected Benefits. [online] Available at: https://ideas.wharton.upenn.edu/research/imposter-syndrome-unexpected-benefits/#:~:text=While%20having%20imposter%20thoughts%20does.

34. www.allaboutfinancecareers.co.uk. (n.d.). What are professional services firms looking for in their graduates? | AllAboutFinanceCareers. [online] Available at: https://www.

allaboutfinancecareers.co.uk/careers-advice/types-of-business/
what-are-professional-services-firms-looking-for-in-their-graduates
[Accessed 13 Nov. 2021].

35. www.ambition.co.uk. (2021). Market Trends Reports for
Professional Services 2021. [online] Available at: https://www.
ambition.co.uk/blog/2021/02/market-trends-and-salary-
reports-h1-2021 [Accessed 20 Aug. 2021].

36. www.momentum southwest.co.uk. (2020). Stepping up into a
management role for the first time. [online] Available at: https://
www.momentumsouthwest.co.uk/stepping-up-into-a-management-
role-for-the-first-time/?utm_source=pocket_mylist [Accessed 19
Sep. 2021].

37. www.spencerstuart.com. (n.d.). CMO Tenure Study: Progress for
Women, Less for Racial Diversity. [online] Available at: https://
www.spencerstuart.com/research-and-insight/cmo-tenure-study-
progress-for-women-less-for-racial-diversity [Accessed 13 Nov.
2021].

38. www.youtube.com. (n.d.). The Essential Skills Series -
Influencing Skills. [online] Available at: https://www.
youtube.com/watch?app=desktop&utm_source=pocket_
mylist&v=N0bOluHqUmg [Accessed 14 Dec. 2021].

Printed in Great Britain
by Amazon

77047352R00153